The Great American

2020 ELECTION STEAL

The Great American
2020 ELECTION STEAL

by

Paula Beverage

* *

Define:
You = Government & Affluent.
Us & We = The People.

My writing style is controversial, tongue-in-cheek, trope on documented acts done by The Bush's, Clinton's, Obama's, Biden's, and their cohorts in Washington "Swamp Creatures."

There's a bit of Law Diction, Urban-Diction with spicy Latin sprinkled in. It is full of common sense on the alleged leadership in a Poem Ditty Style Book that is an artistic, chronological, historic reference up to the Date of 01-01-2021 from We the People's perspective.

It's time the government serves the private and public sector, not enslave us! Government immunities and Corporate Interest have to be stopped! Term Limits for Career Politicians! Investment and Interest Limits! Corporate, Marketing and lobbyist Limits! Usurpation Limits! Overreach Limits! Political Criminals and Terrorist charged no matter how high of an employment position they hold in Executive, Legislature and Judicial Branches of our government. Their lack of initiative to serve and protect our country and the people is more apparent than ever.

This book is about America's freedom and America's fighting spirit, "if we can keep it." Our inherent rights our Forefathers endowed Natural Law to us and scribed in our Constitution. For the people to be able to apply to all these paid politicians "power junkies" who serve us, the people. To remind these wankers that they are not kings, queens, princes, princesses, Lordship, or royalty! They don't get to play that game in America! Our respect and reverie for our Commander-In-Chief, President Donald J. Trump, (A WORKING MAN) as well as the people of the world who are more like us than not, who want freedom and liberty.

WARNING: THIS BOOK IS TOO HOT TO HANDLE and COULD CAUSE COMBUSTION IF YOU ARE EASILY TRIGGERED!!! ADULT AND COLORFUL LANGUAGE!!!

The Great American 2020 ELECTION STEAL

We remember those two Arkansas boys who were adventurous when they went out to play in the dark of night. They were found dead the next morning on the railroad tracks. The locals said they must have stumbled upon your Crop Dusters. That had built-in perforated bellies to drop kilos in the cornfields. Just a little casualty that could have disrupted your supply chain, if you didn't take care of it.

Your planes are filled with crimped rime in parcels that look like Dijon origami. Marked with your logo of a skull and bones You obfuscate your arsenal of death, onto us. You are always in receivership of our losses. We didn't flood our own streets with all these drugs. You dole out dope to our cherished youthful proprietorship. your dapper manufactured pharmaceuticals of opioids, crack, meth, and AKA methadone clinics of "challenged" victims you feed off of.

You're so affable in your mecenas we all pay for and you make your money from. You are emaciating the hell out of all of us and if we don't want your advancements you give us a thorough tongue-lashing. You just have to dope everyone a little for a steady cash flow and an increase in stocks that trade well amongst the wealthy. No one can ever ask you about, you choosing dirty bundles of greenbacks over the needs of We The People.

Your hostile caregiving of grief and misery brings you great enjoyment making us all gravel. Persuasive participation with your big stick of force. That makes us all melt like butter. You are too important to be prevented from destroying the earth, a little lone our lives. You think you know it all. You can do whatever you can dream up. Then you demand us to follow, no matter what!?! You advocate, you know best and if we disagree we may need isolation camps. While you stick your nose in our family affairs and you rummage through our trash. You think you know everything about everyone while your own kid is on crack.

Your exemplification of commercialized drug dealing is gallant. You have MFing Big Brother Reps in empty suits. That walk right into the Doctor's Office to make a business deal of pushing your products. You have one cost to produce then there's the vacillating cost of sales increase to us that are astronomical. It's to pay for your VIP Scholarships, your VIP Practices, your VIP Mansions, and your VIP Memberships to your exclusive closed-mindedness Enterprises. But for us pee-ons who buy, sell, get addicted, lose our families, go to prison, pawn everything we ever owned to pay for doing the same things you are doing? At the only job we've ever known for quick fida to pay for the vanquishing debt, you punish us with. Along with your make-believe staggering stigmas you build out attached to us. Data, Data, Data. Our records are broadcasted, rhetorically. " You and yours' will never see that side of the business." You just hire people to handle it. Pay what you need to to never disclose it. Yours are rich enough to just start over, go off on vacation. Be eccentric, write a movie script of what you did and how you got away with it. You can buy yourselves a new career, with new proposals, on your new portfolio, with a new company name. Your ugly is sealed by the courts from the spying eyes of the public. You help each other get away with it. You will do this for a paycheck? Be at risk of tarnishing your public persona? There must be some aberrant in the government that We The People aren't aware of?

Military, Medical, Scientist, Legal, Political, Business, Accountants, and Industries with all your Professional-ism's that you tongue bathe us with. You are the expert of shoving down our throats your sugar-coated sh*t shined clabber. You have sold out your own Industry's integrity. It doesn't speak well to your intelligence or character with mounding cadavers in the morgues with your names on every body

You spike your team altruistically in opposition to the better good of our Nation. You could have been heroes. You could have turned it all around. You could have put your foot down. You could have healed the world. Peace on earth shall never be as long as there are 1%s that can not be punished when they destroy the lives of the little people. We need to dissolve qualified immunity when our rules do not apply to you. We need a legal separation so you can start thinking about what it is you have been doing to our country! You're causing these rifts, Nationalist vs. Federalist.

Your concept of importance and leadership needs to be overhauled. You could have stood your ground on our behalf. Protect our girl for the next generation from this ginned-up plandimic agenda. You could have preserved our election's integrity. America could have been valorous. But look what you have done with your ill-granted powers. You are the cause of America's disgrace. We pay you to employ us. Let's just stop this. You need to quit us. When you plot against us. Your acrimonyism is fatalism to We The People.

You're kindred of royal over-baron-ism are insufferable Censorsaurous-isms. Socialist, SuppreSSoros-ism. A family of Dictator-Dinosaurus-Rex-Schism-Ship. Fighting is feudalistic. Our government makes love to the ceremonial mien, role play. Your synchron-isms is all for show in your performance of rewriting reality and scribeing it into monument proportions. With the Federal Government GP trackers and algorithms. You are in complete disordinanance as you squander our wealth and natural rights from us. Your procreed aura of imbalanced chakra is shocking like Rocky Horror.

You're after our golden goose, America, and what she represents Constitutionally. In your statutory world of overlord, a person is not a person but an entity. That is where you get equity. After you took away our Live Birth Records. You want to give pre-programmed bots identities with "birth certificates." Your trans humans spam us and tell us if we don't like it we are racist. You are protected by newly founded make-believe, special rights. Because you are more important than the rest of us. You predicate manipulated numbers against us. You controle our choices and nothing is real unless you say it is. Then you have the nerve to call it the will of We The People? We aren't allowed to check the records and we're told to trust you because you are the professionals. We can't even call it double standards when you have no standards at all.

Let us not forget about the Vets you never could find the money for the whole time you held office. You shut the VA's doors, then the Veterans had to travel for hundreds of miles just to see a doctor. So why would we be surprised when you put their dead bodies in garbage bags and dumped them like trash into sanitation fields in the state of New York. Your funded programs always fail us. Someone is always taken too much and to hell with everybody else and their frontline defense services.

You support these "Banker Wars" that send our flesh and blood into the killing fields to spread your uniformed one-world currency. The USA soldiers guard the Middle Easterns' Poppy Flower crops and our President(s) were caught stashing narcotics in our soldiers' corpses. Then you flew their bodies home in boxes. You honorably buried your dirty little secrets after you took your packages from their lungs' cavities. You handed their parents a folded American flag in trade for their sons' and daughters' lives. A militant chaplain said to their mother, "Their sacrifice wasn't in vain."

When you run the government that runs the people, you can make drug deals and take body count, it comes easy to natural-born killers and sociopaths. Power junkies, who are in it for the clout. You pull the strings to our lives, from womb to tomb is Certified.

A system that is simulated by billionaires that have total control of our Maritime Admin. Where you stuff our strawman into a file under our family name with a Social Security Number on it. No one is allowed to have a life without your Bar Brand upon us. Tell-tell signs of who really owns us. You are our father in an absent parent kind of way. Neglect is your middle name. We fend for ourselves with the wolf pack at our heels and we are sure you sent them for us.

You call yourself the "ruling class," only proves we have the inmates running the asylum. You Hunger Game Society. You're a long way from clarity when you're on your higher academia sirer and your pathetic self-important ism charades. The issues plaguing the globe can not be solved by people who are making more money brokering the problem(s). He with the gold, rules... To do what's right is not why you do things! You may need to get your head checked when we start diminishing your cash allotments you stole from the entroproneriers and workers. We'll see what you are made of without that cash front smoothing your way for you.

There will never be another George Carver Washington if education is all you have to rely on. New ideas and new ways don't come from followers. A gifted life doesn't give you superpowers. You have never had to solve problems. You're missing that part of your cognitive. Now let's talk about real life at our level for once. A subject that gets you crumped and all screwed up in your thought proces. We want you to experience it for yourselves. You need a change of scenery down here in our atrum.

Inventors, and self taught, geniuses like Elon Musk are worth protecting. They should be revered over actors, pathological liars and starched collars. If the germination of creativeness and expression is not nurtured and grown to maturity there will be no regeneration. Then the spark of innovation dies. America could look like the rest of the world. Where all the poor oppressed people have no Constitutional Right Oversight to stand on. Their dictating rulers keep all of their country's money to themself and let their people starve to death! Where welfare is a bag of rice and flour or nothing at all. That may be what you have planned for us in the Welfare State of America?

You call us smelly Wal-Mart people as you dine with China's leaders and discuss our communistic future? Because you both agree we have had too much freedom bestowed upon us and all you want to do is take it from us!

Half of us know our way around a Law Library with or without a degree. We can see through your flimsy devine act. And half of us made a conscientious decision to not partner with Big Brother, Big Pharma, Big Disciple, Big Rip-offs…Your empire's doors would close if your profits relied on independent thinkers. We done told ya to not rush our back side! You are about to get deviated. We're called the silent majority that you are trying to run up on. We are our own protectors and you done shook a quiet giant. We ain't going to take your sh*t anymore!

Your the stupid f*ck that paid a college for the same information that we read for free! With an open information highway we all have access to the same things. We can look up the same public information that you can. But we probably know more than you because we have real life experience. We can figure out things on our own. We sure as hell don't need you to hold our hand like an anchor. We hear your partners get disappeared! That means we don't want sh*t from you. We wish we could cause you to have to earn your own living, like we have to. We want you to learn a little trope called respect for your fellow human bean. We'll see to it you get what it means when we see to it you stop making your wealth off of our pain and suffering! You earn more than us, as you take from us, live above us and speak down to us. Where the hell is your off switch? What you say don't mean sh*t to us! You're just a bowl of soggy corn flakes.

Money is politics and politics is money. Money and politics is power. But without our money you would be a nobody! You and your inevitable dependence on our nourishments, are who wants to choose who we vote for? One of the two affiliated parties you have preselected in every initiative of your transposal. It's out of your control is what you say even when you're in charge! You claim we have to pick between your trained, qualified, predetermined candidates that can afford to run in your money league of politics and for us there is no other choice?

The Deep State and our own money make sure We The People that the government belongs too, don't have enough money to even compete in your clown shows! We have to choose between pre chosen players of your choosing on your monopolated game board. How fair play with-in your own air quotas have you followed proper conduct? How many advantages have you taken advantage of? How many of our shortcomings have you run over us with? You get your side elected to take things from us. So how fair do you really think we think you play?

We have hope and the desire to prosper, with opportunities and some free-handed range in this great land of ours. We don't want more than our share. We don't want to live better than anyone else. We want balance and steady progress. These are your fosterling pressure points and you want to bombard us with cost and problems.

You are not on no higher than us plato that separate us other than the plato you lost your way on. No one person rules this Republic where We The People have individual rights! It's time you start answering to the proper chain of command! You answer to We The People, collectively! Now stand down and start doing what is best for our people and our country! And let's put a legit vote to it!

If We The People can not vote into office who we want, then you have already killed our Democratic Elections! It's a good thing for us we have the law and courts for back-up. But we must work quickly due to the poisoning of our well of survival and our stream of knowledge. You are trying to kill America, her thoughts and her concept of Independence. America's pride and heritage, with our world progress, and our ability to lead come from her patrites. Your sh*t is the same sh*t they do in other monarchy countries. You come to tread on her people or you come to tread on our assets? You're going to get a face full of what you think you came to rule on.

Aristocratic trupani wants to be our liaison and all you want from us is a bit of cooperation by us laying down our arms and surrender our God given Free Will to subpar humans. Just let them make all our decisions for us! American's can't imagine that! Government can't give us anything that Bigbrother hasn't already stolen from us! Government does not grant us our rights and Government can not take our liberty! Not in this Nation, B*TCHES!

You try to intimidate us. You're bullies with moldy fungus acrylic fingernails and fake hair extensions. You are about to get your mop snached off of your head! You best know that no one believes you after what we have all seen come from you. You must like it or you wouldn't be successful in this system that is so extraneous over the spirit of life itself. You forget who you are sworn to serve and protect.

II ✶ II

Bet Midler, is an ideological model who beehoover Aaron Ruso's "America Freedom To Fascism," That shows where "they" made-up earned income taxes because it's easy taking from the poor and rewarding the rich. We The People are equity that's weighed by our FICO score. You trade on leverage in your valuables of minerals, oil, arts, automobiles, shipping, lands, products, businesses and precious metals. All the monies that is generated so you can tax it even more! Why do some have so much, "Fancy Nancy?" But, the masses live humbly with less than 80% of what our basic needs are? We all qualify for the government EBT even if we have two of your low skill jobs! You tell us everything is good when you are in charge of our laws, food, utilities, medicians, money, etc.? We have less and less and you live in complete extravagance. So don't tell us you understand the struggle. We have nothing and you have everything and you still ask us for more! You can't get enough from us in your unyielding control of us. You put the old lemonde squeeze on us. You know desperate people will do anything, you tell us! We are pulling, and pulling while your obstruction of us is pushing counter to us. You're only here to fail us.

Our earnings are in the lower 10's of thousands a year, and we can go away quicker than Al Capone if we get caught not paying our tax portions to people who live better then all of us! One dollar times one million is one million dollars and so on, and so on, and so on. Then you add your percentage. Plus, Plus, Plus. These are your rules of taxing and interest earnings that are not in our Constitution! But you and your rich friends with housekeepers and chauffeurs who decide these income enmities for us. You say it's fair and equals out. Then why do you have too much? We are to blindly believe what you say, and ignore what you do to us. While we are in your deprivation tank of never having enough, But you wouldn't know what that's like.

Your Agencies, like the IRS, who brought claims by THE USA vs. IRWIN SCHIFF who died handcuffed to his bed. You really stuck it to that harmless old man. He tried to open the eyes of the people about the 1928 Jekyll Island illegal taxing and banking practice. You had to silence him from showing where excess taken under the color of law may be being pillaged by you. You made him the example of what happens if we think for ourselves. Standing up to you made him a target with "criminal" stamped on his law degree. Taking down a bar-licensed attorney must have made you feel so high about yourselves and your moral slaughtering Departments. So let us never forget the biggest man in our history who stood up to you, on our behalf, Attorney, Mr. Irwin A. Shiff. A great patriot and Author of, The Great Income Tax Hoax.

We are restricted by this Compart-MENTAL-ism Government Torrent and we are forced to play in your Federal Reserve Matrix. We are Alice in Wonderland, and off with our head if you catch us. You are the Queen of Heart hunting with your Cheshire kitty, kitty, kitty. You control all forms of monetary influence and budget what you estimate will come in from us. You like to be a big shot mentally with diplomates. You are so jovial about your decisions that cause the poverty of the world. Your glutens is to blame for the suffering on this earth.

We'll meet you quick if we don't pay you our earned income 13-percent racket to the state where we live, and self-employment will get us a stay in your hospice prison system. Try to home steed a piece of land, or fish without your tags and license. When someone is hungry and has no food. Us questioning your authority just gets you paid. We'll pay the citations or go to jail. You dominate as a dictator, or you will confiscate it all. You always get the last word when you say, "Your way is the only way," and us defending ourselves against you is contempt on your court?

We've struggled to keep what we have and if we fall down or get caught slipping, you're right behind us to snatch what we have up and you take away everything we have ever owned with civil forfeiture. We stand down while you encroach on what is ours right in front of us! You claim that is the only help your way can afford. When you mishandle the people's money someone must pay to keep the regulators and County Courts corrupt.

It will be your rise in earnest honorary persuasiveness. Small cash transactions, sludge funds, expense accounts. You are the trustee and handed the bank cards. You have the codes to our public accounts. You move your way up by your credentials. You claim you know your constituents and how to run the country that you exploit. Knowing what you know is how you got where you are. You greedy robber barons take our surplus and never leave us, none. Then you say it's justifiable because we are all poor, uneducated, and dumb.

Your upper-crust life has you believing you are superior. You run your mouth like a razor's edge across the working indentured engine. You send your Depart-MENTAL-ized Myth-a-Saurus to tax, enslave, and cage us. Your commanding agenda is take, take, take. We are your cash cows that pays, and pays, and pays.

You own the incentivised prison system that are in the high-end dividends when you're in the know. You sit on the board of directors as an investor in the endless Industrial Incarceration Incorporation and the fuller the house the better your interest do. Our lives being sacrificed increase your fruitful bounty. Such insightfulness you have when you're a holder to the business and you make the laws that oversee the same growth bonds? There isn't no one looking into any conflict of interests when you are at the top of the food chain.

You beat us down with mind control and fever-pitch Deputized Authoritarians that act like a gang of Reno 911 Cops on steroids. You force us to run on your tax wheel for a little bit of grain every day, we grind, grind, grind as if there is no other way to keep food on the table and a roof over our heads. We go to sleep and wake up to do it all the same way day after day after day...You say your system of control is for our own good.

Federal, State, and Local are a business that generates like a Company, that we don't see any of the dividends. You keep the earnings, and then we even pay for the money you hand out. Wall St., Banking, Drilling, Mining, Minerals, Investment marketing, fines, tickets, taxes, earnings, collecting and accruing interest accounts so why is America in debt? America would be broken if We The People didn't carry her on our backs. Government is a system of incoming moolah so where is our money at? We all should be living so well as all you fat a*s rats!

You take our cheddar to make you wealthy and you don't care what we do without. You call yourself the master over the laymen when all you really are, are Revenuers with Parasite-a-Duties.

That's why you like to be in charge, so no one can question you. You want to be called the boss and you divvy up the cash. You have a job, you have an oath you're sworn to uphold, and you have a pay cap. Yet you sit on a title like you think it's a throne and fill your fat purses with our stolen coin as well as personal gain from inside knowing, gifting, and transferring? State and Federal legers that never balance. Where is all our money going?

Are you getting wealthier from our ballooning inflation, toppling our Nation? The killer to our Liberty? You are a wrecking ball to our harmony and stability as you canonize our future indebtedness. Our U.S. Debt Clock is a sirmounting time bomb. You spend our money like furloughed drunken sailors. While your elector never crosses your mind. We sure hope you'll had a real good time in your state of conglomerate blissfulness!!! You make life unbearable when your job is to bleed us dry!

You think you're so righteous when you're showing off your asses, but that doesn't make you smarter or more accomplished than anyone else. You're called an entrepreneur for what we would be thrown in jail for. You write the warrants that you serve and execute on us. You are a full participant to us going without. Thieves verbally assault us while you add injury to insults and you always back your sh*t up with a gun. While you walk across us like you think we are escargot slugs.

We think, "you think" you're the Wizard of Oz and you think no one can see who you are. Throwing everyone off your yellow brick road and covering up your tail with drowsy pills, is how you stay two steps ahead. Your buddy system will straighten up your mess and make it appear as though you were never there. We saw what you did, but you will twist the facts and say because you did it, it's not a crime. You always have diplomatic, sovereignty, immunity, and special privileges. You are the government and exemplified from punishment. You and yours don't have to worry about it. You wouldn't know what just rewards are.

Your kind are always changing your names? Your kind are always changing your forum? Your kind are always changing your semantics? Your kind are always bombast on principle? Your kind are always collecting from foreign Entities and Special interests, Promotion Lobbyist Capital. Your kind live Fast and Furious. Your kind always has too much… Your kind is always spun out. Your kind can't figure out how to shift "Equity" to equal out? Is this "your grand" oh-so transformation that's supposed to make you "grandiloquence by governess supremacism?"

Your kind's goal is always who is who on the Forbes list, while the people you serve go cold, hungry, and sick. We'd beg for mercy to your Magistrate for the things you do and get away with. You wear our rule of law like an invincible cape crusader cloak, that the

Constitution does not apply to. We'll pull back your interpretive crime vale you think makes you unassailable, Until we all pick up Pro Se Law to hold you off of us, by counterclaims against you and you can request a criminal stay. We will beat you with the same stinch you have been getting away with beating us with. We The People will break you like an egg sucking dog.

You talk out of both sides of your face, you act as if you care. You say you are the side that wants to get along. You claim you did not start a thing, but history will reflect you own every conflict. You stack deception as a defense to the erratic distress you cause. Your tower of Babel is no Pillar of Nobility. You have nothing but non-scrupulous propositions you force off on us. You cause the denigration of We The People who you are too good to serve. You never live in our neighborhoods. Yet, you bear no fault, you have no blame, your ne'er-do-well is death to the people you knave!!!

Your leadership is heinous. Your implications have been nefarious. You should receive a hanging sentence with your guilt by association. You have no excuse for all your lawlessness. The lesser of two evils, that aspire against us. You are repressive, dominatrix, and 50 shades of rapist. Your scapegoat is Baphomet and the blood you shed out on the streets is never your own. Oppression is not governing, and our government are two-party rapscallions. That is all one-sided. The so called leaders of our country have gone butt a*s wild.

III * III

We have to inspect what is behind the closed doors of the career leches that we pay? You have made all of your professionalism look like a sham. We need a Scrutinee-General for your illegal relations with power and money kickbacks. Full Disclosure with Disciplinary Measures. A need to separate your business from your pleasure? Do you need to clear out the empties from your desk? Shouldn't you keep your personals at your own home with your blissfully gullible partners or would that be an indicator to your office liaisons?

You have been tipping from your own supplies, again. You are drunk on Patron, again. You be dancing on the table tops or sleeping under them. "You are the newest, greatist, edumacated monocracy of expertise of all time in history. Yours are the betterist guess-o-metric spectrum of alternative fake fact standards. You wanting to be in charge is a whole new level of stupid. Can you get you some help with those problems or do you all suffer from the same mind virus diseases of mental decompensation?

Your Christmas parties after parties by Exclusive Invitation, ONLY! RVSP, RESP, ex rel no-tell RITZ. Your 1,2,3 password key that can override a hard drive. It was bought for you by the highest bidder, who bought and controls you and your world of runway models. You're up there. You're a High Roller. You've put it out there before. You are one of the beautiful people, ♪The beautiful people, The beautiful people... ♪♪ They are not always ethical, so be careful what you wish for. They've already tricked your a*s out or you wouldn't have gotten the invite. Handcuffs, whips, and strap-ons are given out as door prizes. Remnants of the Playboy Mansion, which comes with a bazaar of actors/actresses that are willing to show you how to use them, "on film." Pocket pool in the corner like Pee-Wee Herman. A high-stakes roller of strip poker amongst professionals. No holds, no folds, live inter-cloud calls. Webcam Only Fans, Dick pics, Xerox copies of your butt-tox hole painted with lip- stick is an O'Keeffe masterpiece. Men in dresses want their nanny to spank them. Sheltered separation of one's identities. Covert integrity and you're letting it all hangout, cuz you're a wanker, a cheeky monkey, and growing up is not a course of action you'll be taking.

You're wearing nothing but a turbine and a sheet, you're a Natty Chic with a harem... No one parties harder than a politician, financed by Rockefellers, Hollywood, and Silicon Valley's nerdy perversity birdies. With clipped wings in swinging cages. Tweet, Tweet...

This custom coach is built on human tragedy, and it will take you anywhere you want to go, princess. So, what are you willing to do? Take a chill pill or two. This ain't your grandma's party unless you're Barbara Bush's mother and Alister Crowley. Wading through bodies of debauchery. Come on into the duplicity, the water is warm and full of skinny-dipping working girls. They tell no tales, and they are there strung out for the taking...

Eyes wide open you heave the toll and take the stern with no discern. You are a Heidi Fleiss pro. You're focused on the decadence going down on a line of men made of steel! That big iron horse is throbbing. It's thrilling and you feel the rush like a quick gasp for air, "hyperventilating asphyxiation, strangulation" like David Carradine. You take the wheel, you find the gears like a CDL driver. Your goal is on the haul, riding on a runaway rail of connecting cabbies, and powered by a Conductor all night.

Do as thou will be done and the key to joy is disobedience. Making Daddy hard is thy will and money's always a part of it. Abuse does not satisfy your depravity. Too much is never enough! Your gaudium obsession is other people's pain and loss. You're sadistic, you're a bestiality, donkey show mongrels. Kinky Sodomy, Roxy, Foxy, Brony, Furry, is no longer 18 and older. Child cultivating and adult entertainment has no division. Your early grooming is causing violating characters. It's getting concerning all your XXX early introduction to seduction. THIS SH*T IS BLATANT F*CKARY, AND YOUR SH*T AIN'T CUTE OR FUNNY!!!

You will never unsee it so light it, don't hide it, pack that firebox, and blaze those memories as you gain momentum. Whistle-blowing Wu hu slowly fading... rolling, rolling, rolling, cash flowing, liquor pouring, and being paid, coming and going. It's all a little hazy? A postage envelope of photos...And you will do as you're told to, or they will destroy you! Choo, choo, all aboard the Politidicking Campaign Train. SHMOKING CASH because money is no object…

IV ✴ ✴ ✴ ✴ ✴ ✴ ✴ ✴ ✴ ✴ ✴ ✴ ✴ ✴ ✴ ✴ ✴ ✴ ✴ IV

Rumsfeld admitted a day before 9/11 that $11,000,000,000.00 was missing from our Department of Defense and no one could figure out where it had gone. Then the Pentagon was "hit" right where the only copies of the DOD's accounting records of that missing monies were? We all watched in disbelief when 747s dive-bombed the Twin Towers. "Diesel fuel" melted steel and concrete so hot that it collapsed Tower 7? There was no help? Fighter jets' defense radars were turned off. Our leaders had appointed the Air Force to have practice dogfight exercises at the exact same time the bombers went off and planes hit the World Trade Center. This made for a mad flight scramble and a perfect royal flush for the largest massacre of humans perpetrated in history in one attack on America. RIP, our never forgotten people.

Bush and Obama rained down hell on Iraq and airstrikes raided their cities. You targeted Saddam Hussein, and Osama Bin Laden, but said nothing to Saudi Arabia who wired money to the Middle Eastern Terrorist Hijackers? Petrodollars make you a cash king that can reflect all guilt, and no one questions you, and who knew what before it happened?

You patronize Americans with the choke Cheney collar you've put around our throats. Bush wolves bite the hand that feeds you by calling your savage pack Bill the Patriot Act. 2001 you sacrificed our Bill of Rights like rapacious carnivores wolves. Your canines rip through our appendages to gut our First Amendment. Anything we call our heritage will be banned with prejudice. Nothing Native to We The People will be left standing. Everything that we built and put our names on will be suspended and dispersed amongst the wealthiest in your Capstone.

You increased penalties, punishment, and our broken trust after you butchered 9/11!?! It's almost like all this was by design? Then your Commission Report wrote your noteworthiness off into the sunset. A settlement payment to the families of a few hundred thousand dollars to never disclose the memory of their loved ones, again. Now why would you need those claws?

Your Decorated Generals are trained for paral, and they order the Sergeants to send the Privates to clear the way for your taking. You act as if you are compassionate when you march our children off to fight in wars that defend you and your Financial Hierarchy. Bush ordered over 40 drone strikes, maneuvers to take crude oil rigs. Blood, Bombs, and Petro Oil come with high markit increase when you hire your own Halliburton Oil Co. for your profit and gain from the endless wars you perpetrate. It doesn't take a Scholar's Degree to figure out who is f*cking us up the enkindle shaft!!!

You think you can't be reeled in. You are all chameleons, shapeshifters, you're green-eyed envious wolves. Your Komodo Dragons, fork-tongued lizard people. You are not human and you have ill malfeasance towards We The People. You want to watch us fade and not get in your way. You spread nothing but falsity, and density, in all your disparagement. Your oodles of boodles grow by criminal stats. Your chaos runs the world of stolen booty.

We care and look out for friends and neighbors but because you always know what's best for us, you gave us handheld life-saving equipment to entertain the brainless. You own them so you can listen in to our conversations on your Obama TRACfones. We love to gab on your screen. We 411 text a whole lot of nothing that we said, blab, blab, blab, "you don't say," STFU, LOL, hearts emoji…

We are your dimwit repetitive creatures of habit, and you always know more about your "sacrificial lambs" than what we know about ourselves. You round up our flock to fleece us with some draconic tic-tac-toe claim with administrative fees for the sheeple that dare question your reign. Because having a criminal record keeps the sheeple in line. You bark, jump and we say how high. Neutered rams pay the fines to keep the wolf breath off our balls that are missing like our inherent rights. Good little sheeple do as we're told and the rest will get no reprieveal.

You are lamb-ee rulers that cut the weak from the herd so you can use our own BAA-BAA, BAD words to entrap us in self-incriminating discourse. When we had no victim, you filed Complaints by the STATE vs. OUR NAME. We pay the State and we pay the State to pay you when you slaughter us in our own courts. There is no fighting the Government and your titleholders have no losses. Which makes all of us a target. You are an agent of the agent to the agency we have a grievance with. Preemption Masquerade Takers Ball. You think you can double talk us. Your psychosis is on full display right in front of us so go ahead deny it all. We wouldn't expect any less from a perp. You gore us with pitressin. You split us open and stab, stab, stab. You pathologically penetrate us. Your cannibalism craving hew us. Look at the condition you leave us clinging to the edge of sanity. Renderence of your own's blood on your hands establishes where your rank in life is.

Mental Mind F*cks, "paperworks with papercuts filed precariously with questionable grounds of jurisdiction?" Just ask Marc Stevens. Making Record by perjury and impractical means. That always awards us probation to put us on the NCIC registry. With a National Criminal Record to follow us forever. We can only be what you have stereo-typically type-cast us. You mugshot us for your files. You remind us of the things we've done even if we were innocent. You will always hang it over our heads to hold us back. We The People's lives left in ruins come with promotions that make you a higher-class overseer, over the lower-class people. This class is better than that class, and your class always comes first, "at the cost of our country's equality foundation." We will end up like every other region of dystopia. What the hell good do you think you are doing when you punch down on We The People. We shine your shoes for your chump change. That doesn't add up to a hill of beans. We live on hand to mouth pay and you have more than you can count. You beat-up and deprive people who have less than you do? If you could learn to punch up your equity issues would equal out!

You are wealth generators and who do we think we are to breath the air you paid for? You live in an artificial world. We can't afford to live where you live. The lower class mass will always come last. That's the way that it is and that's the way it will always be, with your high-archy-malarkey social scores of stature. Your credit rating is meaninglessness-isms to us when we live where we live in a state of mind of paycheck to paycheck or doing without completely.

Ⅲ ΔЙ̄S KAPPA ALPHA personage of Scholar, Legal Panjandrum, and Identity Politics. Your double talk makes you sound like Idiots. We are to do as you say not as you do? Did you learn all your muck-a-villain in college or does your exaggerated hyperbole come naturally? Your altruistic twisted brain patterns erect nothing but difficulties and barricades. You dispute us, refute us, you ignore what we say. You segregate us accordingly by your potentate. We have to wear your profile. You make crime profitable.

We never know who will be benefited and who will get the drawbacks. How much can you take from us to give to someone else? How much of our suffering has to take place before you can see us? The more you infringe on us, the more you disengage from us. We presumed we're in this together? Then you leave us when we need you more than ever.

You say there is nothing you can do for us. You stalk us, mock us, and you attack us. You rob us, kill us, and you call us terrorists. You say you are our champion as you put the nails in our coffins. You bury us alive if we need to be silenced. We are electing into office super predators with ulterior motives. Half of you are Anti-American. You don't deserve our loyalty, you are not worthy!

You're an impeded influencer peddler not a studied pristine splendor. We could all do a better job than all of you with a spreadsheet and a box of Crayolas. America's Laws and Politics can not be operated by people who don't understand them or just want to choreograph and act a fool in legal tribunals.

You manipulate for your personal benefit! This is supposed to be a joint collective. For the better good of all the working people that contribute. You are controlled and owned by money. Your cities crumble. Your suburbs fall away. When all your structural integrity decays. You do what your collabo say, instead of what you should do! You are so thirsty for our banknotes and coagulum hemoglobin. YOU DON'T LET A GOOD CRISIS GO TO WASTE. WHEN YOU TORCHER AND EXECUTE THE MASSES. YOU UNDERMINE ALL THESE CONSISTENT STATE OF

EMERGENCY(S), AND WAR(S). UNCHALLENGED PRESIDIUM PARTAKE IN THE HONORARY SYSTEM OF THE HOMICIDAL RAPING AND ROBBERY OF WE THE PEOPLE. GENOCIDAL MURDERING DICTATORSHIPS WITH AGGRAVATING CIRCUMSTANCES. THAT YOU WILL NEVER BE PUNISHED FOR! LITTLE-g gOD SAID AND SIGNED, "IT IS SO ORDERED," IT'S LEGAL, IT'S FINAL, AND YOUR FRATERNITY BLOOD BROTHER ARCHIVES SAY SO. YOU PUSH YOUR UNHOLY VIOLENT COMMANDING AGENDA OFF ON US BY ANY MEANS NECESSARY!!!

V *V

Your lip-licking lambchop with floccus as white as Snowden defected to Germany. He was your computer anilyst to your International Security Information System like Gadget. He slipped out on you and got away. What he knew about you, made you want him bad! When you could not get him, you assassinated his character, but you never let him tell us about your criminal implications. The death of our First Amendment, CCTVs on every corner, face recognition, back doors on PCs, 5G towers, and lack of privacy on every mobile device with live Google Map tracking. Sounds like we are swimming in a fishbowl to us!

Your Soldier Manning leaked videos of you dropping bombs on innocent civilians. Reporters tried to tell the horrors of truth by podcasters, were defamed and we were told independent news isn't real news. You said they were unreputable like WikiLeaks and Julian Assange who took refuge at the Ecuadorian Embassy in London to save his life from America that was hunting him down. The Swedish authority clouted a criminal plot to expedite Assange. Chelsea and Julian were both tortured and went to the slammer.

The only crime they committed was showing the world what you all have done. We want to know why you are not in the electric chair for the crimes against humanity you have committed as your team cheers and makes it look fair.

Hussein Barack Obama made 99% of the world's generated wealth goes to the 1%ers. And in 2009 Enron never paid a thing to no one but themselves after stealing their investors' 401(k)s and retirement plans. Obama cashed Murdock out while Occupy never asks Barack why you weren't paying back the people Enron robbed and why Obama spent our money to bell out private-owned businesses, private-owned banks, and Wall Street? No good deed goes unpunished and in return, We The People received the greatest housing recession we have ever seen.

You want to glorify Hussein Barack Obama for writing his oppressive inadequate health care into law, "The Affordable Care Act." Is a Magic Hat Act for Marketing and Big Pharma. With the most inflated price that there has ever been for medicine made by China. Sky-high costly care, forced by law copays and mandatory monthly payments if you were lucky enough to have a job when Berry was in charge. Hussein Barack Obama put everyone in a welfare line. Nurse Practitioners, Emergency Rooms and Clinics are the poor peoples only Health Practice that will accept your Medicare and Medicaid system and we did not get to keep our Doctors.

You had a fleek wealth accumulation account you thought was out of Fort Knox. You spent our inheritance like cash. Mo Monee, Mo Monee, More Money... You hired triple the staff and gave everybody raises. You traveled the world and you had fashion extravagance that never cost you a dime of expense in the 8 years we have known you. You keep telling us what we owe you and the only thing you gave America was DACA.

You had $60,000.00 hotdog parties that you tried to hide out because you only like your hotdogs over 7 years of age!?! Ping-pong tournaments and slumber parties down in a new TBM custom-built basement under the White House??? It matches the Urban Fortress money-eating underground world beneath the Capitol Building.

Washington deemed it the million-dollar hole that we paid for 30 years ago.

Berry Soetoro was only worth $400,000.00 when you went into the Presidency and came out a multi-hundreds of a millionaire. Hussein Barack Obama turned our White House musculus while supporting ISIS agenda. Hussein Barack Obama sent pallet loads of our gold to Afghanistan to facilitate genocidal killing that has been going on for over 2000 years.

In 2012 Obama told Mr. Medvedev, Vladimir's spokesperson, to wait until after the election and you can help Russia to more of America's mineral and land rights that belong to We The People. You may have been in on these foreign infiltrators to our government? Because you proselytize like Redd Foxx selling us back our own hubcaps.

You are such a narcissist. You gave yourself a Nobel Peace Prize while you caused more killing of human lives than any other president. You dropped over 500 drone bombs on innocent lives and their homes. You left these people's lives and land in rubble.

Your smile is so brite. Your tongue has such wit. When you laugh a room of bulbs light up. You are so charming for such a niyamit murderer, of the people you owe your life to. Then you sent boatloads of our tax dollars to build back what you bombed, and blew up? Did you pay for all your killing, that is never-ending? As we pay for you and Michael to go on permanent vacation.

Och Och Barack bought a multi-million-dollar mansion within blocks of our White House in 2016 for Obama-Gate Headquarters. Three houses from Alifantos that allegedly have Pizzano delivery tunnels and are making the sauces, in the basements? Does Obama, Cowl, and Cluny prefer penial walnut flambay because there are more pictures of you with white alfredo and pizza? That must be your white privilege at the top, that lets you get away with so much? Oprah and Tylor Perry must have it too? You'll pay $10,000.00 a plate of pie? At your curtailed handkerchief club's gatherings, there will be kids in the pools for your enjoyment whether they like it or not??? Those children in your telling photographs look horrified and tortured! Why are all you grown non-natural parents always grooming other people's children? Little Asian girls tied up in crates or in bikini togas? "Toddlers in Tiaras," are these little kids your Water Bearers?

Isick Cappy had a kill switch with Attorney Lynn Wood. Tom Hanks took a picture of HWY 66 roadkill while you took a Medal of Honor for Obama? You have no redemption when the signs said, The End. You slay it. You quail it. You make sure it doesn't come back to bit you in your a*s ever again. We The People premiered it like we are all in a transfix daze. It cost Jone Rivers her life and she was always on your side?

Now your ex-fact-o-men that wants the keys back to our White House that you complained about while you resided there... Your Michael said under her breath, that you hated our American flag. Chicago doesn't want you and we have all thrived since you left.

You need to go back to help the people that you share a bloodline with, in Kina where you were born, because you are not a native to America. You can take that Michael, and your boyfriend Jesse Smollett with you when you leave. An African sabbatical would do you, boys, some good.

VI * VI

The New York City Clinton Hillbillies were trending leaving office. You loaded D.C.'s furniture into a moving van and blamed the workers when you were caught. You had to return the priceless cherished furnishings that you had stolen from our White House. But that won't stop Hillary from wanting to come back over. You're bold in your thievery.

You can take Hillary out of the hills of the hillbillies, but you can't take the hillbilly out of Hillary and the Hamptons is a long way from Little Rock, and a short adjacent bridge to Washington, DC. Hillary's forever home if we can't put her in the Big House.

Hillary and Bill knew how to leave the presidency looking just broke enough to not have to pay Mrs. Jones for sexual abuse charges. But Paula gets a nod from us, she is the only one of your victim's that put you on the run and got some buckshot return fire back to you bums.

You weren't that depleted leaving D.C. because you pulled together your petty cash to purchase a new mansion in Chappaqua, NY, where Hillary ran to be the Senator for a state you were not from and you had never been a resident too. You would have had to have run against JFK Jr. for that seat, and you were not expected to win.

You've been caught election tampering in Porda Rico, Venezuela, Spain, Haiti, and several other little corrupt countries."That don't want to see you again." Hillary doesn't run races that she doesn't control the outcome. That's when JFK Jr.'s plane had to be fished out of the Atlantic Ocean less than a mile from Martha's Vineyard. After the President, the Clintons, and Podesta finally sent out the coast guard 12 hours after Kennedy's plane's distress calls. What a loss to all of us, and sorely missed John, Carolyn, and Lauren.

It's all a conspiracy and everyone is plotting against Hillary, Bill, and Podesta who are a perfect trifecta-666-partnership. Horned Masonic Crips. You are so in-favor with the Zion Gang Members.

Hillary loves her powerful men, you're on film vacationing and snuggling up with the wallets of the wealthiest of them. You are so close you have gotten several of your personal, child-loving friends off NAMBLA charges. You're a Dixie Mafia Chick Globe Trotter that has finessed your higher knowing from side-to-side to stroke down any conflict in interest, uprising.

The perks of being the manager of Wall St. and getting pay-offs for brokering the electrums looks like inside dealings? It would be a crooked way for you to make money, if you weren't an attorney and made a career of shady trading while shadowing lawmaking over the issues that govern your own Portfolio Interest. That's where you got your professional name Crooked Hillary, Esq.

Hillary had high influence and was able to redirect the government treasury to your personal expense accounts from offshore private interest subsidiaries. Then it's used for your personal purchases or write- offs on your taxes and anything else you think America can buy for you.

Good is not good enough and was never good enough for Hillary. You always wanted more than just to be a Lawyer, Senator, Secretary of State, and First Lady. You plotted to be the First Lady President of the USA, "Those terms are used facetiously when spoken!"

You are always willing to scorch the earth and everyone on it if it got you what you wanted. If things don't go Hillary's way, we could be Arkincided with questionable circumstances to those conspirators' demise. We have nothing but love and respect for Seth Rich and all the lost truthers, as well as Bill's only son, Danney. No greater sacrifice was ever made, and no American flag will be draped on these heros caskets. They will get no Honorary Notice from the world they tried to save.

Your personal gain was your only target at the demise of others, is no trouble. Your path was paved with human remains of your victims as you crushed them with legal precision. Others lives aren't worth much when the least of your gore can be cut and discarded. No one is more important than you. We wouldn't want to end up a number on the Clinton Body Count List.

You've had your say about the rise of oppressed women's rights lately after you held three of the most powerful positions in our country and a law degree. You made your husband Governor and President. You've metastasized high offices by being a killer Defender. You had the power to tell most men in America what to do, but you never helped any woman in your life. You couldn't be bothered to help any women's issues in the 70 years you've been alive.

When you were quasi president, you shut off the food stamp to the needy families and passed the most stranglehold ever on welfare reform in 1987. Your Human Service mangling was so restrictive on the people that it had to be rewritten and re-reformed without Rodham's input, across the backs of the poor.

Hillary sold our mined chemicals to Putin to make nuclear and the money went to the Clintons Foundation, not to America. You said you were under sniper attack flying into Iran when there was a cease-fire order. Why would you have your own hired guns firing on yourself?

You are the expert. bribes, bets, bombs, and trade embargos. We have lost track of all the weapons and ammunition that you have given away to keep these warring countries warring... The same warring countries where their children can break down an AK 47, a machine gun, or bazooka faster than most adults in America. Now that's F*CKING scary!

"What difference does it make what happened in Benghazi," said our Secretary of State, who would not send help to our men while our Embassy was under attack. Because you are f*cking heartless. Then you were Federal Indicted and you committed Destruction of Federal Evidence when you Ejus onus, by destroying 33,000 emails on your server and Blackberry. You had unsecured Res ipsa loquitur National Security and The District of Columbia Servers at your Colorado and New York houses in the basement. Where you bleach bit, highly sensitive Secured Intelligence and finished every motherboard off with a hammer and sickle. Not to leave out your questionable barn burning in New York.

In Deposition, Hillary acted like she didn't know what "C" meant on Classified Documents and she said, "What, wipe the server clean with a cloth?" You can have your own a*s wiped clean, but you left a toilet paper trail that is stuck to the back of your clad polyester pantsuit and it's following you everywhere... like your old pictures where you're wearing your shitty draws or your kid making millions from her diarrhea trench mouth. Professional sh*t retailers. How do you show your face in public? LOMFAO OUT LOUD @ U. Retire already, sell your books at your much-o-dollar public speaking events that you have to pay extras to support you because you are not popular with the people… Nobody chose you, so put that in your next furbelow novel!

Wiener and his wiener pics were held at the NYPD. Aberdein, Weiner's wife, and Hillary's handler are so close they share with each other our countries Security Classified Files of the most Private, Sensitive Intel, and no one had security classification level approval. But Wiener did have an extra copy of Hillary's 33,000 destroyed emails and then some.

Aberdein's real mother runs a Terrorist Refuge Boot Camp right here in America and just a side note these are also the same people that in their country they cut out little girls' labia's. They sell their daughters. Allow child marriages. They also exile, and execute adulteries women and openly gay people. Hillary did not support gay nuptials until the turn of the century, but Bill said Hillary was a female Casanova. She chased more tail than a stray kat strut. ♪Get your dinner from a garbage can,♪ and you called all of us a basket of deplorables. Hillary decorated a Christmas tree with crack pipes in our White House reminiscent of your original Arkansas Razorback Business of bringing drugs into our country.

Bill coheiress a Cuban cigar in the Oval Office while being pleasured by Monica Lewinsky, and Gennifer Flowers did Hillary's consummation job for over 20 years, but Hillary shared a law practice with the Scientologist Founder and Chelsey is an identical picture image of L. Ron Hubbard. Talk about a holy mind F*CK and now you're in bed with China!

You contribute nothing to us then you knife us in the back, for your own benefit. You say one thing when you want our vote, then you turn around and take away everything you promised us. You tie our hands behind our back. When you take away our rights, you take away our choice, you take away our voice, then you come to take our weapons because you wouldn't want us to be able to hold you back when you trespass against us. like Ruby Ridge or Waco when you and Janet Reno burned women and children alive. No child's lives sacrificed is too great a price to pay to be successful, said Albright while you murdered half a million children in the Middle East!

When we observe the justice system's abuse of your discretion. We are left in shattered tattered misswonderingment if we're dealing with bigger criminals than the poor person wearing your County Correctional Dept. jumpsuit? Dawning a robe or a title does not make you honorable while you destroy people's lives. You are the people-funded institution that doesn't have to follow any laws. Laws make you money and that money comes from We The People. You are no problem solvers. Stuck in your credulity and no need to change it, no matter how many lives it claims. Your prisons are filled with our fathers and mothers that will never be coming home. While juvenile courts and child foster care suffer overload and all we ever wanted from you was to be left the f*ck alone.

VII * VII

The Biden Crime Family's Godfather always takes a cut from the offshore business investments, floated under friends and family alliances. You've been up to the same De La Fedia Press Extortion Business where you've been taking half from the foreign affairs of your son's and the "Big Guy" gets 10%. We have trust issues with your profiting from our misery over your mistresses in every port, around the world. While you are betrothed to America. Your oath forebode your betrayal to that bond. Your peers won't even look us in the eye and say the words, you are cheating on us. Makes us think you must all be involved. You represent America, before the world and you have a big hard-on for Ukraine and China.

Your Chinese concubine is problematic to America's security. You've been compromised, and that is a conflict of interest when you work in our government. You have been caught selling political influence and trading favors for your personal profits. The peripheral of you using your own son as a go-between in a high-stakes game of money laundering. It's very cavalier of you to have your own son holding your bag! We're starting to see why Hunter is a F*CKING JUNKY!!!

Quid Pro Quo Vice President Joe bragged you held a billion dollars from Ukraine's President as a bribe to get the Justice Shokin fired, that was investigating Burisma Oil Co. Government plots, influence peddling, money persuasion, and it's just a coincidence your own "son" sat on the board of directors at Burisma making millions of dollars in foreign trade deals, at a job where Hunter had no experience. You don't even speak the language or have a degree in oil and gas or in business? Nor did Hunter spend one day at work, directing the board of Directors even though he flew to Russia over 40 times aboard Air Force Two with V.P. Joe. But Joe didn't sonder about the surmising income you both shared coming in from your new forgian friends? Joe didn't talk to his son Hunter about where the money was coming from or just what it was for because that would be inference!?!

You are the Ra Ra RasPutin joke on America that has caused us shame all around the globe. We aren't going to stand by while you sell tickets to you exploiting our country.

On the CBS interview, Hunter said the last name Biden brought you a lot of privileges no one else has, like Plausible Deniability. You have a job to follow up on. We don't know, maybe you should extrapolate from your witness list? Possible, someone's statements like Bobulinski? Did you calculate the plausibility of maybe JoBamagate? Just saying? The Biden's are your opps parts and good luck with that cover-up?

SOOO JoBamas Deep State, CIA intervened to stop the release of Hunter's laptop until the 2020 election was over because of how it would have looked to America and the world? Why is it not our business to know what kind of Burning Man detritus you are going to put in our White House? Reporters that wouldn't report on the Biden's "discretions' ' are culpable in Deep State cover-ups? The theory of the conspiracy that our Government, Hollywood, and Silicon Valley could project Minecraft MK Ultra on We The People is just too far out there! It could cause hysteria if the truth gets out there! Telling us what we can think and controlling the masses is your job and not a bit biased!

That smart, charming, toothless young man Hunter and that nice old geezer Joe Blow had all those pictures of orgies with hookers sucking like a Kirby vacuum cleaner. Everyone is freebasing at a Biden gathering. Gaggers, Gaga, you're no Lady, even if that is what you call yourself. When you blow glass dicks better than caroling wassailer. You trill, and trill, and trill for days. and this is what you call a good time? It's more terrifying to see what is called fame. Cyclops Mother F-ing Monsters with raw meat fetishes. Bleeding, feigning, needing for your satanism hemophagia.

Open drug banks, blood banks, sexual trysts of self indulgents, self mutilation, self sacrifice, and self importance of humanitarianisms. Surmising on the unborn's consumption? Eating Sushi off corpses? You always have clean-up crews as rough neckers to handle the carnage inorder for you to have the purest of your proposals. You think this makes you a Master Class? You have no postulation beyond vanity.

Is that a child trafficking tunnel map tattooed on your back? When 3 million kids a year go missing? What's up with those kill-rooms, and bathtubs filled with blood? What makes you think your shit doesn't stink? Why are you carried through the streets as if you are pious? You drop a duce and sell it as gaggling caucus impressionism... You are Holy dribble. You represent reptili-ism disorderly Fashionism. Your entitlement runs rampid. Rich people with your unruly kids are rotten. You have the give me, give me, give me's, at the cost of someone else. You can not see yourselves. Your flesh is like caustics. You reek of sulfur and having you in high positions of importance and power is like having Jimmy Savile and Satan babysit our children!!!

Dr. Jill, PHD. in Phys-quackery, will put a bleeding-heart spin about how life has been hard for poor Hunter. He's a full-grown adult victim in every situation he finds himself in? He makes his dad so proud is what Joe said. He's had everything given to him for doing nothing. Just look at his Oceanfront Mansion. All of Hunter's privilege frees him up to negotiate private broker deals on crack-alley, in-between world dealings with world leaders. Who is always trying to collect American Businesses and National Security Secrets? With a few little trade-offs from the Big Guy. By and through legal means, "of course" with the boss's attorney son Hunter. It's all in order to take care of the Biden family with a few little nefarious favors. When you think you're above the law. Cash exchange transactions don't need no govt. documented accounts tracing you or your drug habits.

He went to law school so he doesn't pay taxes. He doesn't need to have an NMC registry or International License as he jets off to make Universal World Negotiations as an Ambassador on behalf of his father... He's the smartest man Joe knows and there's a lot to that, that all of us will never be FYI about. Jobama Gate has gambled them/their/they's presidency on it. The whole Circus Court of Congress and the Dubious Democrat Party has thrown their support behind him. Petti Pelosi said she has one just like him. What could possibly go wrong with the choices that you are making for all of us? As you question us with your poker face and you spend our money like fiending addicts!?!

Hunter has law firm organizations that make his decisions of personification, and a stepmother to legally dope him when the family needs a little extra from him. The FBI acts as his private security to track down his thrown-away pistols and laptops. Then they cut him some slack with a little admiration of subsistence enabling.

No one can say Hunter doesn't do his own Stuckey research and he knows "drugs" and "dancers" are extravagances that he has "special needs" for. He has spent a king's ransom on blow and escorts as a learning curve as an Alps Speed Racer. Motel Rooms are getaways with DoorDash Delivery. When Hunter can't be found for weeks at a time by his own family. He makes his hush-money payments regularly for his alimony, his palimony, and his some on the side straymony. The law is still out on the DNA of all his children while Hunter burdens the weight of the world on his shoulders...

So what's a few more grams going to hurt him? What could Hunter do that Hunter hasn't done before? He shags rockstars and crack whores who are the same person. He's had twins, triplets and your little sister, like Billy Idle, and sometimes to mix it up, he will have himself a hunnypot. He films himself narcissistically. His children will be able to see who made them and how they got here because he recorded their mommy's too.

The paparazzi idolize him along with a couple of young school girls. The newscasters write love letters to him. They lionize him and say they adore him. MSM act so snarky like their brains are fried on acid if we want to know, "what's really going on?" They have no clue if it's pestiferous when our Vice President/President has a drug- addicted, sex addict, and an exhibitionist son that has no acalate of expiriouns pulling down millions of dollars from Cold World Countries that you tell us to fear!?!

Nothing stops a Biden Member and your full pledge to Faustian. But at least We The People don't have to worry about the Bidens being in denial or Jobama Gate pulling the wool over the eyes of the American people?!? Now let us say no more about this if Hunter's daddy wins the race that you've put the fix in on. Tactical Interference!

You must forgive our sinasicism just because we know we would be locked up in the clink or strung out in the streets for all that cheating, stealing, and drug indulgence! But not this newly fraudulently elected illegitimate President Biden and his criminal son Hunter, that has seen more catch and release than our Southern Border.

Hunter left his wife and kids to disgracefully temporarily get with his dead brother's wife and her sister. That's how they support each other's opinions, feelings and parmesan binges. In the Biden family, uncle-dad Hunter running around in front of your children naked torching a steam roller full of black and yellow, is fine until the public finds out. You live in a White Rock Castle that was not built on integrity, and we sure hope you got what you wanted cuz you f*cked us and everybody royally!

The Biden Cancer Research donations never reached a lab to find a cure. You have never helped anyone, not even your own terminally ill oldest son that died as your shell businesses profited. There's more money to be made if people are sick. Wealthy people's world "Foundation Funds" freely received is better spent on the living. You have the perfect cover-up when you run a cash quasi company that looks like a charity.

You and Jill have exed-exes and family you owe apologies to for the compromising situations you have put them all through. You have shamelessly and pompously shown off to the world. You have tried to pass your vial off on the universe as normal. Apparently, counseling isn't a strong enough dose of infliction for a spun-out-of-control addiction?!?!? For America's sake, it's a good thing that the Biden family ain't got no monkey on their back! You haven't made anything better in the 49 years you've been in politics, just ask Anita Hill when you mishandled her allegation of sexual misconduct against Clarence Thomas. When you tried to keep black(s) off of our Supreme Court. And what about what you did to Alexandria Tara in your campaign office and the other 7 women that accused you of your own pro-esk sexual inappropriateness? Being the boss doesn't make it better when you act any way you want to.

You're Chester the molester, you're a predator with power. You take group pictures, and you pull little girls close to you so you can cop a feel and sniff their hair. IT'S CALLED GROPING, and you are so grotesque no matter who you are! That's just creepy old uncle Joe... He's such a good guy if your deaf, dumb, blind and you don't mind if he touches your children?

Those are not gaffes, those are laps of sanity when people talk like you, when you said, "That son of a b*tch better get fired, or you're not getting the billion dollars, just call Barack. You would take Trump out behind the GYM and beat the hell out of him, You was going to kill a bad a*s dude named Corn Pop with a steel chain but you didn't know what his real name was..., Poor people are just as smart as white people..., you know all about cockroaches..., from kids jumping on your lap, and you love kids crawling across you, cause where you were raised they like to rub your hairy legs down. You have gone into senile rages and attacked anyone that asks about Americans having rights or we want our jobs to stay in the USA. You're 80 and still doing push-ups. You could win a race, "that's rigged..." You're good enough, you're smart enough and people like you, "in your dreams!" "Everybody is Ummm," "you know the thing"??? It is called the Declaration of Independence!!! You should know it well as often as you have broken it... You are one gear away from dementia and stuck on "pause." If you can call that speech at all?

You would pretend to bring yourself out of the basement and get propped up by Mainstream Media like you were campaigning for the 2020 presidential election. Other than the embellishing news crews, no one ever showed up to hear you.

You're a broken-down Marky extravaganza in a dying old traveling burlesque show. It's time to draw your final curtain call and take your tired a*s home to Scranton, permanently.

Biden's handlers ran your campaign so you can just stay at home. When they would call for a lid, you thought that meant you were going to get a delivery by one of your son's friends. No one needs to worry because when Biden is President the people and their children that donate to Biden don't get drug tested, "What do they think, they're on crack?" "Come on, man" ...

We're not saying everybody in govt. is on drugs, we're just saying all the drugs end up in our government. So maybe it is time to start hair follicle drug testing Doctors, Lawyers, Bankers, News Reporters, Teachers, Engineers, and Government employees, and all the Administrative Agencies because something is definitely wrong when you're acting like you cannot see all this fool nunnery at the top!

Your decisions affect everyone's life hold below you. And you don't seem to be accustomed or equipped to be elevated without a safety net for us. You have betrayed us. Who has ascendance over these ruthless rulers? You are a mutiny to We The People and our

Country. You lost your love for us. You don't need us any more. Shit's done gone raw dawg and no one is following the law? It's time We The People step in and take our power, wealth and dominion back from you! While you wear your cardigan with a hard-on and we gonne-a put you in prison!

You have overstepped your boundaries. Who will protect us from you when you present yourselves as greater than us regularly. Regardless of the fact we hold title of ownership to this Trust Account held by the United States Treasury. We The Peoples are the Equitable Interest you are sworn to! You have broken the beneficiary ties as our Trustee, in this Breach of Contractual Duty, You disrupted our peace. You uproot our base. You beat us with your blunt force instruments to have your way with us. When you're taking what is ours you say it's anti-anthropological for us to not agree and think the same way.

You're a spy for the other guys that want to destroy our way of life. You don't want us to own a thing. You want us to have an endless struggle and debt makes us beholden to you. Yet, you gave away our intellectual property to China for nothing in return. Our Trademarks and Universal patents are also China's and that means we can't even own our own inventions.

You arrested the Hamman's and Bundys because you wanted to run them off their family Ranches so you could sell our land to Asia and Russia for them to deplete our uranium? Now we find out Bill Gates owns more farmland than anyone else in America. Isn't Gates messing with GMOs, meats, crops, and vegetables? Maybe there won't be any farms and ranches anymore??? What else are they phasing out and we hardly notice or hear about?

Mom and Pop retail shops are no more because they can't compete with one man's empire, Amazon. Our stores and restaurants were closed down, with boarded-up windows and our jobs and businesses disappeared. Where we come from are becoming ghost towns. Then you took away our "Made-in-America" Wal-Mart, and mass produce our products that we buy are stamped

"Made-in-Shanghai." We think we are all getting hung-hi in these government deals. Just know we are all replaceable and Biden told us to learn to code if we want to eat while we watch our countries' services thin out because foreign manufacturing and labor is cheap. Chop, Chop…

VIII ✷ VIII

Are you invested in on America being successful or being toppled? Big allotments of our money that work against our own country. Exemplified from our Constitutional testats? Dissension to our rule of law? Who has wavered these Electronic-ism communistic puritans creeping in and taking over. Are you investigating who has been paying for this feudalism? You seem to be working against us, and not with us?

Your "EXCELLENCY" will go down in history as the vilest debt thot politicians sense the conception of America. You spend our finances into a negative balance. You rolled over the world debt clock times one thousand! You're the conjoined Siamese twins Hillary and Nancy on a JoBama leash. We've all seen your legal trickery. You use our money against us. When you're the biggest criminal of them all.

Do you want to turn over our apple cart in a paradox. Destroy our people? Are you aiming at our symbolic eagle to put her on her back? Implode America from the top, all the way down to the bottom of your roughten barrel? Government bailout The United Nations by depleting us till we have no more to give? You have run our country into the mess that it's in, by exploiting our drudge vs. reward system you thrive on? Behestent to the founders of our country who had the principal and fortitude to separate this land of the brave from the tycoons and barinest, who rob the poor for their paycheck. You want to claim our accomplishments as your own? You want to swab away our ancestry, sterilize our history. You rich snots that believe in human slavery want to preach down to us.

People that think they are better than other people are not good enough people to call yourselves an American. You do not represent the beliefs of her working class people.

We know you wish you would have been born with a dick, instead of always acting like one. You're always having to rub one out real quick cuz no one else could find it, with a magnifying glass. Y'all should have been indicted when your computer was hacked the first time and you were part of the strategically planned attack on our own embassies in Palestine.

Obama overran Turkey's borders with immigrants to break their country and they were our allies. They are the least crazy country in the Middle East, and are secular. Obama dropped 22,000 bombs on 5 country that had nothing to do with 9/11. Why wouldn't you extend the wars that threaten America when you paid and armed our opposition against us? These are just the things we know about. Top level war crimes, torcher, and espionage. You hurt America so much. There must be a special place in hell for your wickedness. You are a multi-headed limp dick demon Bael, with little bitty Chine's dragon penis. You need little bitty tweezers, to beat it. You have Big Eagle phallus envy... You are America's number one enemy!!!

You're so selfless in your self-gratitude, where do you find time for your subjects in all your bigshot hoorah? You spend more time getting your hair done and coordinating your tailored outfits while your governing job has been stagnant. But don't you think you look good!!! You put the simpletens in isolation and distancing mandates. You're so important that your assistant writes your itinerary. You have to rush through your saloon and salon appointments? Brunch mimosas and a few alcoholic beverages in-between meals on the job don't cost you anything when you're the CEO of Congress. You don't even pay for your own bad habits. You take it out of your business expense that We The People pay for. You are magnificent at being better than everyone else. When the pressure is up and your sh*t blows. You rain brimstone down on your subordinates' and they fall in line and follow because you sure as hell ruined the lives of better!

When Nasty Nancy walks, we all feel neck-breaking discomfort to see a catheterized 80-year-old alcoholic stumbling around historic hollow marble halls in 6-inch red bottom stripper heels. You look like a street walker caught in headlights. Hey, turn down the hi beams! You make a spectacle of America and yourself.

You're always popping out of the top of your darted camisoles that's pushed up on your corset to flash your old boobs off. You're musty, you're crusty, to put out that kind-a fringe benefit signaling. You think old dusty Bush Sr. is still around, giving you what you are wanting. You think it's cute being self-centered, while you sit on your money pouch being useless.

You're rusty and fussy, you drag around doing nothing! You've gotten away with accomplishing the least that you possibly can and still collect a government paycheck. You are none productive. You lay down on the finish line and refuse to cross it. We only wish that Nasty piece of work Nancy would stick your gourmet ice cream where the sun does not shine. That should fast freeze your ole push-pops off in your matching subzero temperature chiller that cost more than most of our houses.

Your plenitudes are bountiful. You think you are delightful. You have your own world you live on, and it has nothing to do with the people. Country Clubs, Nautical Clubs, Islander Clubs, the beauty is abundant if it wasn't for these bottom feeder humans on your earth. Georgia Guide Stone says to minimize population down to 10% of what it is now so that should take care of your population control issue. Your bloodsucking, reptilian peoples in a One World Order Club, and all you want is the whole earth and Universe Dominance. "It's a great big club and we ain't in it," said Carlin.

You want to rid your world of the poor, crippled and elderly that are so unsightly. You like to service us out while we are DOT and hot then discard the remainder. You have never had our interest at heart, and you want our country to fall apart, "as Cali has since you've been in charge." We know you're so rich you don't need your job as the rest of us need our jobs to keep shoes on our kid's feet.

We can't buy basic staples or afford to improve on our accommodation. You have your wealth stacked in vaults to accumulate as you pass it back and forth to each other through your tight, slimy little safe holes between your infinite living key partners, with your stockpile growth plan. Upside potential you, downside risk us. You quean, you posture your holier-than-thou lifestyle in opposition to us.

You're a big shot, hoop-la with your pokemon people. You live on Farmville, and Candy Land is raining crypto? Billions in lotto and you have people that are not good with their money paying for all this fantasy that makes the poor poorer and keeps the rich richer! The poor may be the game the rich are playing. The world is designed for the rich not the poor and you take advantage of it. The more suffering, and devastation there is the better "YOUR" lives are.

You don't like any of us having our freedom. You tell us we are all impure. You tell us we are all f*cked-up. You want to cheat us of our value. You want to separate and race bait our beliefs. Drive a wedge in between our families. You want to monitor our behavior, thought police our flavor and audit our relationships. You subvert our interracial culture. Condemn our genealogy and discriminate against us if we love too much. You want to deprive us from our inherent birthrights as if it were your lifeblood.

You give out dope and call it an aid by a Federal Government Program? Look how well the people you help are doing! As they bed on park benches with the pidgence. You let drug addicts and permanently schizophrenic people run our streets and commit crimes in broad daylight? Full homeless encampments out on the sidewalks. You have tent cities in our children's schoolyards. And being a tax paying citizen will get you killed or robbed by the vagrants that skwat wherever they want. We think your way of doing things is to pit us against each other. The ones that have a little have to fight the ones that have nothing. This constant engaged bickering makes us all a nuisance after so many well-check calls. And for protecting ourselves and our properties you can ice us domestic-izers cause we are all so depraved amidst the crazies in the state of despondency you have caused.

You take what is ours away from us until we have nothing left. You lock us up if we try to work, provide and do what it takes to survive. If we call the police for help, against you, makes us the criminal? We live in a Police State! So how are we supposed to back that blue up? You better hold to your Missionary Oath. You work for the better good of the American people and the rich do not own your service!

IX * IX

Actions are louder than words and you are showing us that you are the fascist resh dureri de anus, that you say everyone else is! Haters like to spread hate and we can't tell you a thing. Haters always shame and blame. Haters like to lord their way over on others. Haters say they know more than they do. Haters like other haters, and haters vote for Clinton, Obama, Biden regardless of the things they have done to our country, our families, and our world. Megalomania war criminals are hater's heroes!!! Haters are going to hate on the innocent, regardless of atonement. Can't save a hater from themselves.

You are a communist when you beat up kids and old people for wearing a MAGA hat or for just being Caucasian. You have shown us your dissident tolerance when you want everything your way. We have seen what happens when you don't get what you want, you'll take it out on us!

Do we really need these people that we have to pay to be a leader? Shouldn't you be able to pay us if you want to be our boss? Why do you have a salary or any financing that is a financial conflict of interest to the position you are elected to, to protect the people's interest? We pay for your housing, clothing, dining, and outings so shouldn't you have to cease personal holdings. Your earnings and spending should be suspended while you have a duty to us? Where is your business's financial freeze while you hold office? Where's the pause on your profit portfolio? Shouldn't you be successful, secure, and/or wealthy enough to carry your own weight! Your needs should be basic while you are participles in the people's government? Maybe you should learn to live by your own means. You should have a budget. You shouldn't get to live better than your poorest constituents. As a goad for good. You are supposed to live in your district with us, not in spitefulness to us because you rule by Corporatocracy.

Things are a mess from hiring people that need to be financially coddled, compensated, and contributed to, to work at your job. Being a parody of authority over other people's rights as a uniformed human wrench. You screw the nuts and bolts to us as a Regulator of COGs.

You boastfully brag on how good you are at power driving our lives into the poor house. At your power meetings with your power brokers, as you play the power games you sold your soul for! You think you're so important with full entitlement. When you are supposed to be a public servant. How can you serve us when your needs are so above ours?

Shouldn't you be humble and open when it's your sworn to endeavor to operate the chattel corral that oversees what belongs to We The People!!! You are not royalty and you should not be meeting with anyone and their money, "personally," publicly, or privately. Big money should not be in your pockets, less there be a mousetrap set. Industrial interest should not be taking precedence or left to their own means to grow so ginormously. You should not be an investor to Companies you make laws for! You should not be leaning your ear to minor discretions and to the wolves of Wall Street. Corporations should not be able to silence the private sector, by buying you off! You are a serious conflict to our grantor-ship. That belongs primarily to us. "WE THE PEOPLE" are "WE THE HOLDER." We are your rival to your personal interest. Your combative Childishness vitiates our rights! You seriously have a defiant disorder. Are you trying toreinvent the wheel? Can you come up with some of your own ideas? "KISS" keep it simple stupid! You are highly suspicious.

You rag on your competitors' authenticity as you promenade your untruths publicly. You are completely unethical and total phonies. You don't wish to remove your chains to separate from us? You saunter absolute control over our lives with paid Martialized and Militarized intimidation and manipulation that stands on grounds of fraud. Your fasten is a lie because you don't own us. We are owed no less than a fair share. You're third party mastery of mastering us until we pull rank on you. We are the Master of our own lives. You can't control us. You can't get what we say. You don't speak the language of bare get by. You're in your own tomb of doom calling for control. You're just the frontman for the Great Reset Master Plan that will control all of us. When you do away with cash and bitcoins. We're not allowed to own gold. You steal our intellectual properties and we will own nothing and be happy about it!

You think you should be celebrated by name recognition from your Commercialized, Municipalized, Politicized prominence. You forget who you break your bread with. This sh*t has done gone to your head. You superimpose your will off on us as you say it's in our best interest. Your smugness is so ugly as you look down upon us. You think we are all too ignorant to figure you out! The only people that believe you sadly, are your own followers! You don't speak on behalf of the rest of us. Your time has come and gone. Your Honor and Valor is questionable. You can't stop yourselves from picking through what is ours. Scavenger buzzards lick our bones clean like we were never alive, as another pregnant moon waynes, and tides come in. Nature is not yours. With your new non legislated face of government, and we are about to go old school on ya!

You need to be patted down with a flogger to trigger your disloyalty entrapment garrote. We want to loosen your ties. Massage your knots and rub your kinks. Get a grip on your scrag. Remove your hands from our scruff. You are so rough, rough, rough... You need to relax your maxed-out-ism from all your own exquisiteness. Take your tiara off of your head so some blood can circulate cuz you done lost your minds, up in here. Dress you down a bit. Alleviate your restraints. Try to let yourselves breathe to drop your heart rate after a fat habanero to cure your case of sassy-a*s disorder. Wash your sarcasm out-your mouth with a bottle of Tabasco sauce. Let you cut your snafu attitude on some Merthiolate and give you some cod liver oil for your whining and snibbling. Sir Knight you on the top of your crown with granny's wooden spoon. Now that art to fix ya up, for a while. While we send all ya on your way and dock your pay.

X *X

You have pasted the tambourine around more than Harry Kristna! You're the pinnacle of money raisers. Charities are popularity pageantry amongst the exalted ones. Rich people's tax exemptions have to be made to look like they're something they're not, just like the people running them, and no one in charge is trying to expose the truth. You do not believe the people need any extras, and you are always trying to bleed us out of every dime. You run a wooden nickel susu nonprofit that helps no one but yourselves to everyone's hard-earned earnings. You are a grandioso superfund mega collector of other people's worth, and to hell with where it left us.

You are always in an agonizing, frantic mental state of air-humping master-baiting aggression. Stirring up big deception costs big bucks. You get your return by spreading fear, and fraud, far, and wide, hark the reception. After Lobbyist, Marketing, and Commercial ads you have nothing to show for where the money went. You have done nothing other than plastering your own face everywhere that will print it or broadcast you, and you are looking like a great big bill that America is tired of paying! You have no accolade that you helped anyone other than yourself. The rest is just enough to get you an offset of any debt.

You're a headliner directory. You're the modern-day Pythagoras. You're a three-dee deity that the tip$ at your appendages are collected from the big-top revival trickery. You recessed the spendages back to you, yourself, and yours. You make hundreds of thousands of millions every time you make insider deals and then you have a public speaking event upon the issue, and you get paid again. You have too many built-up assets, investments to ever fall, but you only earn one hundred thousand a year?

Why would you need to even work? It's as if your job is a front? Espyonish paid, la-connection. You have hundreds of millions of Lil' friends and no dedication to us. We've heard we need to look into your husband's longshore island shell man businesses, and your son's secret euro e-commerce setoffs coming from foreign countries. But we'll never know if Biden is in Office. The people that are incharge of our country are the Central Bank and CCP money manipulation operatives. You want to screw us and be an old philanthropist around the world?

Who are you taking orders from and who's side are you on? Why do you want to be in charge of us? When you can't eventell us that you like us. You can't cut your own pay rate. You can't stop the "donation racketeering." You can't cap the cost of campaigning. You can't block Corp. Lobbyist. You can't halt marketing costs and increases. You can't catch the Deep State. You can't fight your own cheating. You can't change a f*cking think, least of all your f*cking selves.

You will singe the eyebrows of anyone who breaks the code of Democrat Handbook of bizarro conduct. You'll throw a belittling tizzy if anyone asks you "why the people can't eat or have relief checks through the lockdown." While you distribute OUR MONEY to save your rich friends in blue states when they can't afford their own luxurious decadents?

All of you need to stop talking about feeding the hungry children when your diet is Spirits, Xanax, and sleeping pills. It's going on 10 months later, hey Boozy, Prada wearing Pelosi, you didn't budget to feed America's children, and you lost their parents their income. You shut the world down because you think you're the only one on it, and everyone will eat when you allow it!

You're a cold-blooded reptile, your veins run pure ethanol, and you breathe pomposity. You hissed like a snake when you said

America's people's needs and their families being able to be fed depends on who the president is?!? No one is going to get paid or eat if Trump is in the White House is what Petty Pelosi said.

Nasty Nancy used willful evil intent with your malingering stall tactics. Thanks for getting into the stimulus negotiations and getting the people what we needed when we needed it...Such caring, timely work you do in a state of emergency... "NOT!!!" YOU B*TCH!!! Leum Helms ain't got shit on you!!! And once again you failed us!!!

Shutdown is not an option, it's ordered because you are in charge of drumming up this false flag plandimic mission agenda. You've been put in that position to cause chaos so you will make more rules if we can't follow the first rules you've already made up. There will be no recovery and the Millennial Gen X, Y, Z will have no employment while y'all pass this ungodly debt off on us. Then we'll lose our homes like when the govt. and banks took our family farms during the Great Drought that caused the Great Depression. Don't think they won't do it to us again! We will all be homeless, without work or food. If we continue letting these human-eating wolves guard our pork barrels. Till there's not enough, then they turn on us all.

You have cross massages with the CDC, and the Red Cross missionaries are on standby to burn and bury the millions of deceased bodies falling in the streets dying like it was smallpox in the 1600s before antiseptic. How stupid do you think we all are?

CDC is going to have us all in a bread line. If you don't open our country back up and stop passing your referendums restricting our abilities and liberties. Stores with signs that say we're only allowed one roll of sanitary towels in the middle of a deadly pandemic. Did you forget how to make toilet paper like you forgot how to land a man on the moon?

The Fractional Reserves and Central Bank will not save us. You make your wealth from our suffering and prices going up. Any debt the rich encounter is passed off on us! You do not carry your weight and you do not pay your way. You anime-money for yourself. You did not get where you are because you are a good person! You got where you are because you are willing to take part in the culling of ours. You do not care what happens to us as long as your coven is safe! You will do whatever it takes to keep you and yours above the rest of us.

This COVID-19-plandemic mission agenda is an abuse of your power!!! You need to stop telling us what to do when we didn't get COVID-19-plandemic pay with 6 months of compensation like all the other countries received in 2020. These mental cages you have built right here in America for Americans doesn't bother you because it only affects commoners. You don't care how many peasants live without shelter or provisions. But you'll send the hospitals our money as a silent incentive promoting the writing of Corona as the cause of death when a person died of natural causes! In an effort to get the tallied total to a National Federal Level of Emergency. To have a scaled scandal, sometimes you have to combine and crunch the numbers for good measure.

Legislating isn't forced mandates and authority doesn't mean scaring the whole human race into restricting oxygen to our brains. Who gave you the right to force us to wear a face loincloth apparatus that cannot stop your virus? Towels and tea cloths are condoms, now if what you say is true? Telling everyone to wear a mask is as cerebral as telling people to wrap a dong in a paper towel to stop sexually transmitted viruses and pregnancy too? If you are right, why would we need latex?

Don't get us started on where your hands have been? Medical equipment is to be worn once when you are in a sterile controlled atmosphere. When a mask is handled repeatedly fungi microbes are spread everywhere and back into our pulmonary. You are restricting our free breathing by forcing us to suck our own air. We think you're causing adult SIDS Syndrome and you're psychologically damaging our children!!!

We should be able to take away your air and let you turn your favorite shade of blue while we decide what to do about you! Of course, we're going to give you some air right before lack of o2 kills you!!! We don't want you to die, we just want you to stop thinking for us!!! We want you to know that comes with consequences when you break your oath to us.

Are China and other countries making these triage masks that we are buying and being forced to wear? Don't they wear masks in China because of their toxic air from having no factory regulations or human rights laws? If everybody must wear the theatrical mask everywhere then aren't these masks causing more litter and pollution than drinking straws?

You have no business making rules for us when you go to work so hungover you wear your watered-silk matching pantaloons across your face, and you call it a surgical mask? You surrendering, your Freedom of will, doesn't mean we all have to! Who are these arbitrators of these pie in the sky rule-making from classroom monitors and intrusionists? Do you decide who has cooties or doesn't have cooties? Who can be friends and who can not. You are so third grade with your transmuting references of idiocy... You are a disgrace to the Medical Industry. Your followers have Stockholm Syndrome, and just because you obey you think we all have to? You don't like your job of dealing with the public and you wear a mask to hide behind because you hate people and should not have a job serving the people!

You are losing us our natural herd immunity with all your scientifically made variants of virus dubieties of a cold and flu. You have a BIG L on your forehead.... How has the dumbest of our species been put in charge of leading us? You do not own the air that we breathe! You are smothering us! You people have Munchausen Syndrome! You are sicker than all of us and you need to be locked away in a moratorium! For the better good of the world!!!

You have grown men and women shuttering to your commands to "mask-up" whether we are sick or not. Even if we have a healthy immune system didn't weigh in on your "add to the strife" COVID 19-plandemic mission agenda, even if there is a 99% chance of recovery. All you are doing is virtue signaling disorder with a white flag of surrender across all of our faces. S.O.S. AMERICA!!!

Now the Constitution is deferred, and everyone can go around self-policing anyone else that didn't get aboard the false flag plandemic agenda. That comes with a "Patty Wagon Ride" from Big Brother's MK Ultra... Self-Destroyers of rationality is not a phase of idiolatry. It's weaving its way into our society. CDC-approved narrative and Fauci funded, SUBMIT, SUBMIT, SUBMIT! All the Power Junkies don't think We The People are smart enough to think for ourselves. You are the new creator(s) and you have dismissed God, The Messiah, Genealogical, Racialogical, Archeological, and Scientifical with your Fantasi-a-rifical. You've put our life support on critical notice. Dispensations are choices of the wealthy! And to hell with the people's first 12 Amendments they will be suspended due to your illogical unreasonableness!

You have cuffed the world with your fantastical scheme to rule the Universe when you made the whole plandimic-up!!! This SH*T made you minuteman money, selling your inox-cinox concoction(s), and Government funding. Notoriety from depriving the people. You've been making this sh*t up as you go along. Now our spending is in the trillions. You are nothing but cucks and American ain't your B*TCH!!! You are just F*CKING clowns and idiots!!! Take your self-serving servitude with all your degree(s), all your falsehoods, your false attitude with your false prudence, and all your false authority against our free will, and use it for some kindling!!! Americans are about to give you some what-for! If you come to take what we love... Our Freedoms are non-negotiable, and we shall not be surrendered by a bunch of sellouts!!!

You don't care how long you drag out this false signaling of your sirens of distress, distress, distress all around the world. You make us sick, you mixed this virus up in a Petri dish. You turned it loose on us. COVID-19-plandemic mission agenda is not your first run amuck incubus from Dr. Tony Bologna Frankenstein Fauci! Did we ever find the source of AIDS in the '80s? And it was the US military that created Amthracs in the '90s. We do know Tony was there for both of them?

You were told to stop working on Gain of Function in America, so you packed up your work and moved it to Wuhan China. You've been paid to secretly keep working on your Global Threat that transmutes animals to human Geno-receptors. Your Hypertension Cardiology Coronavirus Diseases with clinical features and correlating bits of bat soup from wet markets, are considered cause and effect of this mutated and manipulated plandemic?!?!? Now America is paying you millions of dollars to be the expert of your own professional negligence to your redheaded stepchild that escaped from your financially funded laboratory! This is your #19 gremlin Chinese sniffles?!? Why have you not been held liable for your Wuhan baby that mutated!

You are so hubris, and we are supposed to believe you after Bird Flu, Swine Flu, Tuberculosis, Bronchitis, Ebola, AIDS, and Cancer when you sent our loved ones home to die. No one rolled out the red carpet or untied the Gordian Knot for them when you mail the custodial party the debt-owed payment plan, and where we can pay the rest of our lives but will never pay that medical debt off. We have no relief from our losses from your Fibonacci scale. There is no inoculating breakthrough to this day, and instead of damaging our Natural immune system why don't you stop playing in labs working on biological warfare. You can't even cure a common cold so let's not try fooling each other! Your facade is given way to the truth beneath it. This is about your power and your control over the people, not a man manipulated spore.

XI ✶ XI

You have no moral compass and loyalty is not your strong point. You called Trump racist then Petty Pelosy visited your friends in Chinatown, LA. You said China is always welcome and you fought Trump when he stopped flights into America from Asia. You have called China, who is "A World Superpower, A Developing Nation" and you have been sending them our money, to help build up a country that is millennium years older than we are. Our govt. charged them nothing to bring their products into America, while you also let them charge us for incoming products to China. They sell their goods for discount prices to undercut the world market after they stole the Universal World Patent(s) from the little start-up artist. China leaves everyone broke after the U.S. Trademark and Patent Office doesn't protect the American Inventors. What do you think old Ben Franklin would think about that!?!

China owns interest in all the world's investments and has managed to make money from Americans' third-party dealings? Ghost Traders. But our accumulative US Debt is mostly owed to China? That is an around-the-world swindling operation! We are damned if we do, and we are damned if we don't. When our own countries' international deals are not protecting Americans.

Biden said that Xi Jinping genocide and enslavement of their European neighboring people are scions and it's the Chinese ancestral tradition to take a whole nation from the Uyghur Natives. China is a Communistic Nation. Who won't let their own people leave their apartments, homes and workplace. Absolute Lock Downs! Latches on the doors of turrets that are strung with nets to stop suicidal employees' life taking attempts. Disparaging, despondent lives of indentureship to the Industrialized production of enslavement. To a controlled people, being restrained is normal! Having choices is scary! And running is deadly! They live with no food in your sprawling urban sectors as you look down from your citadels. Poverty is getting real, real quick and we will never know how many have died from it? China knows how to keep its secrets!

NY Govt. Gorgon Cuomo sent the susceptible elderly to the infected nursing homes even after President Trump sent a Naval Medical Ship in 48 hours to stop you from killing seniors. But you refused to use it! Nasty Nancy wouldn't sign the Relief Package for the American people that needed help the most while we watched you eat, drink, and play in tropical paradises.

Red alert restrictions tell us we are not allowed to be around each other. Holidays, Death and life celebrations were all canceled. You told us all to social distance, all the public schools shut down and you put our nana and papa behind plastic. You said no one can go to visit adult living facilities. Then you even wrapped the mall Santa in bubble wrap. Which keeps our people and children in a perpetual state of hysteria.

Your kids went to private schools that stayed funded and open. Your nana and papa were kept up in in-laws' quarters with private nurses and housekeepers that came and went every day. While you flew chartered jets out of Washington DC to go on several travels with your staff, coworkers, associates, acquaintances, and loved ones. You can have parties and gatherings. You and your friends can go out to dine at the French Quarters. You and yours can enjoy mixed drinks on private DiCaprio and Branson beaches, island hopping because you're immune to the problems that plague the gloomy everyday provider. You told us we weren't essential workers, so we didn't need to work at all. Essential to who, Nasty Nancy? Because when we don't work, we don't eat or pay our bills, and that's essential to us! You closed the world down with your trojan horse that you rolled in for the takeover.

This lockdown was only supposed to be for 15 days. 3 quarters of a year later everything is worse, not better. It's been one hell of a curve as we all face planted. You told the common people good luck surviving and to stay inside our houses. Don't go outside or we'll be arrested. You barked, you growled, you brow beat us down. Then you backed it up with local armed forces! If your virus plandimic mission didn't kill us, deprivation and separation damn sure will.

To survive, we all lived on rations!!! Small-owned startup Businesses couldn't keep their doors open and weren't allowed to have customers to earn a living, so we lost everything!!! But online shopping, box store outlets, and foreign investment malls are all doing well and are going to make it through this hardship. Nasty Nancy said, "Some is not better than none in stimulus money." Because Nasty Nancy doesn't like Trump. Your slaves will suffer for your divience. You didn't care if anyone ate or had utilities on in the year 2020. You called getting an offering of pay, crumbs and you hovered those crumbs away. Your voracious, slide of hand, and cover-up(s) have cost us all irreconcilable injury. Your deceitful leadership has Damaged our Nation!

The facts are you write pork bills and refuse any leeway for the people's needs. If you are questioned about your spending of our money, you bang your fist on the desk like old Mr. Burns and you shuffle out of the room. You're a linchpin dictator, not a proficient negotiator! This is not your house to shut the door of communications. You hold the executive power as leader of the house, and you turned your back on us, Nasty Antwanete Nancy when you reduced negotiations to non, which is non-negotiation, Eeyore!!!

You drug your donkey honkey a*s in and out of crisis meetings with lovely Mr. Meadows, and you Hee Hawed the whole way. Then you refused to meet at all. No peace offerings were accepted. Compromise insulted your lack of integrity. That's how the Democratic House caused failure to perform when you have 300 million people that are depending on you to do your F***ING JOB!!! B*TCH, WHO DO YOU THINK YOU ARE! You don't act that way in our house of the people. When we need our job, we do a lot of things we don't like to do, but we damn well do them anyways, Nasty Nancy!

No one asked you what you like or don't like in a life of servitude. It's called the People's House because you don't do what you want to. You represent us and what our voices have to say. You are not our governess or a saint for your people's needs. You have proven you do not fight to indemnify the wishes of your electorates. So why is America stuck with you and your Breach of Duty to us? And why aren't you being forced to step down!?! We The People need to be able to hold special election(s) to remove this Sedition! This is Treason! You have manipulated us and your power! You are working against the people! You have put yourselves before us. You have put America last!

This is an illegal cease of our country. You spread this virus! You called for this plandemic agenda, you shut down America and every other country you have control of. Then you would not sign a relief bill. You failed to assist in aid and services. Now we would like the Justice Department to do its duty and escort you out of our Capitol

Building! You need 86ed and permanent ejection!!! Write you a pink slip and mark your sh*t up in the history books.

You caused this epidemic of false flags. You caused all of this plotting under pressure. You shut off living happily ever after. So now if you can't leave our house peacefully then we can damn sure do this the hard way!

Illusions and falsehoods are low-bearing fruit that should not be sitting in a high rank of our Executive Branch of Government. If you question us again, and again without thinking first is a clear indicator you have no answer to anything! You need to be spoon-fed and to take a seat in your highchair. You've turned us all against you when in solidarity you wore white in support of you all being Benedict Arnolds! The Speaker of the House tore up the State of the Union Address. We all shook our heads, and said, Petty Pelosi is drunk on her power "again." You all should have been removed from office for such ficence, reproach, and ethical offenses! Does your self-love cause you to detest America? Your hatred is showing from behind your virtue signaling!

Your dentures don't fit in your mouth, and they are popping out. You're always grinding your gums like you grind our nerves. You're a flatulent cud-chewing bony old ewe of a performance. When you talk you look like you've knocked a few back. You slur your words and can't present a cohesive sentence like your jaw is packed with chaw. You're a spitting, pissing llama. You think you are a non-educated, non-commercialized jailhouse lawyer and witch doctor. Everything you say is Orion lunar Osram communicator approved... We are sure there is a mental ward somewhere that is missing you. We would all feel safer if someone would 5150 you sooner than later. Transmission...Ex-Na-LZP-NP-Out.

Take that gavel from your hand and stop your frothing and whaling your arms when you try to speak. You're always hand signaling the Vulcans. While you motion for oxigen? Your presentation looks like you're having a stroke? You may be seizuring? You need a mask, muzzle, and restraints. You suffer from rambling delusion and alcoholic poisoning. Shouldn't we know what meds, and substances that you're taking when you work for us! That less than a shot input of estrogen pheromones, and testosterone, is from you mixing your hormones!!! And probably a few more drugs that we don't even know about?

You have a lack of working gonads, and you look weak as f*ck. You're showing signs of thin skin and scurvy of the people, mouth diseases. You are pompous in your self-inflated ego. You think you are a supreme-ism primadonna. You are higher and holier than your maker. Thou's pretend Xyzzy Jurisdiction is a side effect from your Adderall and your liquor induced hand-cocking.

You are rigid and you want to keep your distance cause you don't really like us. You are implementing iku-boss and you think we will let you run over us with your shocking loss circuitry. You're choken, you're broken. You are morally bankrupt, and you need to be put out of your misery. You need unplugged when you can say whatever you please but we all have to watch what we say or we can pay your citation like a curse jug to your Metropolitan Judicial ATM machines with auto-withdrawal payment plans. We don't even have to be present to get f***ed and robbed by the Man. This Virtual Reality, make us not feel a thing until it's all done and long gone.

XII ✶ XII

You use OUR MONEY to bail out your dollar-raining good time buddies when they misappropriate/misspend "OUR PUBLIC ACCOUNTS" called "OUR TAXES." You told Blitzer, "You feed the people!?!" You have fed no one and "THE PEOPLE'S MONEY" feeds the people and you. You are Govt. Welfare leeches." The Govt. is Socialist whether the people are or not." YOUR REVENUE is generated by you being a F**KING TYRANT, not from you respecting and representing us.

Those are OUR MONEY ACCOUNTS that we pay into, and Petty Pelosi needs to be told who's a*s you need to be kissing. Petty

Pelosi needs to be told who's A*s you should have to kiss. Pin the tail on the donkey, to remind you who you work for and who this all belongs to. Not the Corporations you screw us over for. Petty Pelosi needs to pucker up to every little bitter copper penny… One hundred little ones add up to one great big one…When you get what you have coming to you!

Apparently, we have jobs, or you wouldn't have OUR MONEY to scwonder! We need you to marginalize OUR PUBLIC ACCOUNTS for the paupers that cannot help themselves. Those that are in the cold sleeping outside on the sidewalk just feet from the front door of your California's Capitol Building.

Your Chiquitary spread of appetizers and cocktails aren't what is being served in America's cities' food pantries!!! Bush Jr. tried to fund the Churchs to feed the poor. The separation of Church and State gives the govt. an excuse to not help our communities., Reagan stopped funding the psychiatric clinics and facilities. That put the mentally ill and drug-addicted human beans on Skid Row, at the same time you started a drug war on them. Our streets have been war zones ever since.

They're Invisible People, and you have never cared about them before so why would you now? You could not even see or smell your shit-lined streets until you paid 200/300 dollars for every signature you harvested from the homeless camps and welfare lines. You didn't care if they were American or not!!! Restraining the poor is easily done by the Democrats' irrational restrictions being plotted against us.

The Plandamonium panic button has been hit. With paid-for scientists and security to back you up. Rational Ph.D., MDs., our families' Doctors and nurses were stopped who tried to speak out. They were fired and silenced, over you and your COVID-19 plandemic mission agenda being completely blown out of proportion. You weaponized your narrative by exoneration. You wicked, evil, Nasty Nancy, Susan Akins is a nice girl up next to you.

You are all Privilege, Prejudice JoBama Gate fledglings and you called for unity for all the Mulatto American people at the same time you called for a race war on the average white man. BLM, Black Militia, ANTIFA, W.E.S.N., and Central Gangs, L.A. Riots, Guerilla Warfare, Black Panthers, NAACP, ACLU, and the Moore's. Samurai Democrat recruiters are wolves in sheep's clothing, and even you have outdone your own utopia of double standards. You can trace your roots with the KKK from 1854 all the way to Biden Poobah and the Grand Wizard. You wore white sheets with fire torches and "Black-face" Trudeau, Harring, and Northam. The whole Damn Democratic party is Jim Crow, Patty Duke, Helter-skelter, Reverend Sharpton with Tawana Brawley. You're always stroking racial tension, yet you're the party that failed African descendants while you only pretend to represent them.

Emancipation Proclamation of 1863 by Aberham Lincoln. The 13th Amendment, Civil War, and the 1776 Revolutionary War, where our ancestors fought for America's Liberty and Rights. Right here on these grounds so we aren't all prejudice and racist or our grandparents wouldn't have battled their own relatives for your freedom! Brother against Brother because not all white people had slaves!

XIII * XIII

We all saved all year for our Christmas cheer. Daddy swipes Mommy across her rear cuz he knows who pulled this soiree together. We all laugh, and everyone kindles in peace, love, and harmony. MmmMmmMmm the smell of Butterball turkey in every kitchen. We all have a full plate and there is more than enough to share. No one goes hungry at our family festivity. If someone is far from their kin, they are welcome to join us. Pull up a chair, and make themselves at home. No one should be alone for the Holidays no matter their beliefs because the Lord made us all equal, and we are to judge no one is what our mother would say. Let us all take time to speak on what we are thankful for, amen, mazel tov, pass the cranberries, and dig in

Something is wrong with your thought process when you are willing to do ANYTHING for fame and fortune. Hollywood can kiss our grits and rump roast. Sop that up with some biscuits and gravy. Wash it down with a big glass of whole milk, Mmmm, delicious is our cornucopia of abundance. Even for those that must eke out an existence, are better off than most just because we live here, so there is no excuse for this spiteful vengefulness. America the land of plenty will let you choose for yourself regardless of controversy. Our liberties shine freely from sea to shining sea and in the soul of her people. Our freedoms are as broad as our imagination and doing good when no one is watching is how we do things. We're not always trying to grab the spotlight in our day-to-day lives.

We'll roll up our sleeves, to fix what you have broken, you do not deter us, and sacrifice does not scare us. We're going to get through all this unnecessary mess you have created. The real Americans that built this country where we live. Not the "entertainers" that play while we work. You're the ones that never can be counted on, you never come early or stay late. You've never seen a job to its finish. You are completely useless, and your shortcomings should not be our higher standard. You being catered to has made things worse. America and her people will not be overtaken by the "Corporate Antonyms Fundraisers" that have more dollars than sense. Nemo me impune lacessit thugs have infiltrated Hollywood and our Government. When did our political office become a "buy-in" exchange market, in return for a seat of executor power to our country? Where We The People's votes no longer matter? Apparently, any ole Soros or Koch brothers with CCP interference can buy some of you. They'll have their way to control our tech programing, Ethernet, intellect, infrastructure, agriculture, elections, pharmaceuticals, our treasury, military armory, nuclear secrets, and weapons, as well as our White House? None of us will have a say when you have your way with our Republic. China's flag will be flying over Washington, D.C.! We want to see you talk to China's General Xi Jinping about your LGBTQ, BLM "special rights" over SIMP white people when we are all in labor camps. FYI

"General" means he is not elected and China's not a Democratic Electoriente Country! So, you better stop acting like brats on your own while you still have that choice. When you take other peoples rights, you'll die by the same double edge sword.

The Dem's placate the people to get elected. Your monopoly of democracy is a game of spinner-dilation. You rule by self-pity. You are a glutton for punishment. Your moderations have no tolerance. Your gratification is s'mores-orders to encroach on our God-given privileges. Then you take away everything that we have known since the earth's first birth and conception story. You won't let us be proud of our ass-whooping families and our own legacies. While you have made the whole world hate America because of your endless wars of intransitive-ness on impoverished regens who lack LaRousse or fortitude against you! Now you want the United States of America's Government to establish anti-white-ism against the forgers of this Great Nation? You go tell that story to every Foreman, Laborers, Militant, and Immigrant that helped to build her because someone, in everyone of our families are from somewhere other than America, and they love her like we love her.

These are our regions, major metropolitans, and our little hometowns. These are our city folk in our molting pots of our country. These are our county roads, highways, interstates, and overpasses that join together all the travelers, truckers, workers, builders, makers, caterers, grocers, shakers, and crafters with the ranchers and farmers both large and small, across our vast prairies and Plains. The land in between are our forest, mountains, and tundras. With range all the way to our beaches from Portsmouth Oregan to Portsmouth Massachusetts. We all will aggregate alike in unison. When we put our hands in the wind and extend you a single-finger salute of victorious triumph like we are World Wide Wrestling for Trump, and we will Cage fight ya! You go woke you go broke messing with the heartland of the United States of America.

XIV *XIV

Cancel Culture bankrupted the NFL that has mostly black players, who were all carrying lucrative contracts. When your teammates don't get paid. You should be ashamed to show your face. Talk to the hand about what you got planned to do, you never did what you said in the first place! Go walk it off before you get tossed and don't come back when you are blowing everyone's opportunity.

Kaepernick took a knee to protest the Prison Industry's unjustness, but Biden wrote the Crime Bill of 1994. Three strikes and you're out, is death to our life sentencing even if it was misdemeanor drug deals. Bush's, Clinton's, Obama's, Biden's, Harris's policies have filled the prisons with the indigent to full capacity. Your era incarcerated more black people than any other time in history. You built correctional complexes and halfway homes, but you did not work on prison reform. What have you ever done for the poor communities or any of the American Industries?

You made us as poor as possible with very little reward to participate with you. So don't question us when we break ranks with ya! You separated our American families, you left us broken and limping with our homes half empty.

Did you name a star in the sky in memory of the severed losses with the people you work for? While you "wished" you could have helped more? But that "Wish Bill" never made it to Congress's floor as a proposal plan the whole time you sat at the Round Table? Kamala held inmates past their release dates to have a free labor force for your chain gang mentality when you were the Cali, DA.

You defended the pedo priest and wanted to jail mothers for their kids' truancy. Harris's laugh is psychopathically covering up malice like the Joker Heath Ledger's ascent into madness. We're not allowed to question you and your abuse of power and discretion in the seats you've held? That would get us a stent in your Reprogramming Detention Center, for questioning whether you won the 2020 presidential election fair and square or not. You were canceled in the runoffs and did not make it to the primaries. It's like you're forcing yourself off on us because America didn't want you.

What kind of shotgun wedding is this? How quickly can we get it annulled without losing our lives in the process?

You were subordinate to California Brown, and he got you to the California Attorney General Office where you signed off on that Dirty Fraudulent Dossier and now you've been made our VP by Default? We couldn't make this SH*T-UP! You were in acquiesce to a 70-year-old married man because you suffer from mens rea. You f*cked your way to the highest office in America held by a woman. You'll be taking that Hitch'em corner post. You went whore-a-zonal for your career to go vertical. Red Light Districts of no-say none material. You slept your way to the top. You're a complete savant. You know no shame. You haven't learned a f*cking thing. We have no respect for you and your burning inferno of reality. You're what we try to teach our children not to act like.

We want to ask one question, when do these posers, pylons, and putasos get vetted before holding any taxpayer-funded offices or Administration positions? Intramural assessment by colleagues that never makes it in your files. We would also like to add a rule and that would be that lethargic, lying, kleptomaniacs need not apply to the USA Government, but that means you all have to go, and we would need to start over in the governing assembly with people who are not career politicians and "supposed, so called professionals" with money-motivations that run contrary to our interest. If any of you was any good at your job we wouldn't be in this mess!

Senator Bobby Kennedy is dead, and we can resubmit Term Limits for review because thinking these career "contestants" can be trusted to resign on their own is as stupid as kissing a rattle snack on the lips! We are in a need-to-know relationship so where all do you have your tentaclaws into? AND YOU ALWAYS NEED TO BE REMINDED EVERYTHING IN GOVERNMENT IS PUBLIC!

XV *XV

Google, Facebook, YouTube, Twitter, Amazon are Mammon Demons. Pied Pipers who mislead the masses while you make so much revenue, you have your own tax agencies. You are your own sovereign countries, like Windsor Castle or the Roman Vatican. The richer you are, the less law means to you. Are you buying your way into our government? How many millions have you donated? Do you have political influence? Have you been paying for favors? Dividing America? Diluting our integrity. Waning our strength of unity? Do we all have to bow down to all your money, be your yes man, and pretend to like you?

You have colluded and have not followed Jurisprudence. You cannot see what you refuse to look at. You tell us to believe what you say to believe when belief is void of evidence. You are the new Sheriff in Netherland and there will be new laws of do as you say not as you do. Everybody better cow-down and shut-up! Close our doors and don't be outside. Don't talk to our neighbors. Don't let the sun drop on our back side. Because that could come with fines and jail time. A couple of seniors may get their kneecaps broken! Consider this our only warning!

You hide behind a cable line with the things that you say, you do not live in the mess that you make, you've never been shut-down and shut-up, like you would have if you would have said that to our face. You are always telling us what we are permitted to share. You're Tonya and her bodyguard at the Olympics, and you're taking that no opposition platinum, you don't care who you have to wack-a-mole! You'll take out your own teammate. Because you are Wacky, Wacky F*cking Crazy!!! You have already gone completely mad!!!

You can't have it both ways. You follow Journalistic Law as a Publisher or you learn to mind your own business, Gladuce Craves. You are not rational, you have double standards. You should not let what other people like bother you. You're the aggressor so stop pushing upon us. We are about to yell you're a molester if you force us to surrender our will to join you under your big soggy wet blanket of tears! You are the teller of these authored news stories. Those are your personal opinions, not Newsworthy Commentary. Your convoluted reporting is the cause of America's limitation and splintering. How you choose to slant your pen against a person is how you divide the people.

You sold us an antenna while you built the only satellites. Your radar towers send out your microwave static so we have to make forever payments to you to F*CK us out of our money every month. When you crank out the air blitz on your side is all that can be heard. You're in full denial of your delusional acrimony. You are a butcher and maneuverer of the actualities and there is no other side when you drown it out. We are going to have to say we believe you are leaning heavenly bias with your manipulation of the facts of what is deemed viewable material by you hacks. You are so bass-ackwards, independent newscasters are going to have to call Project Veritas because you need Alpaca Retracta legal mediator services against these big brothers kink links, and MSM folly Data. Hutzpah…

You are acting like Justin's daddy, Fidel Castro. You are being dictators. You are the Empirical Rulers of your own astro-no!no!pro Ethernet world. You are so dense, you can't pick up on what is being put down by your own ratio that says you're losing viewership. Your investigative journalism should be fertilizing Pansies. You need the facts and percentages explained to you. You apparently don't understand slides and scales. You are as repulsive as the book burners of the Great Library of Alexandria. They could not hear the others and they caused the loss of treasured knowledge from our ancestors. You set us behind centuries in developmentry expansion, because paper refuses no ink from your poison quill, and the victor's side is all that we hear. When your radius spans the globe, you can silence the MF VOICES OF THE LITTLE PEOPLE!!!

We're not allowed to see and hear what you deem inappropriate, or we'll do without completely, with strikes or our income looted. All our work goes missing. You erased your opposition. You have supplied us with the facts we can intake. If we argue with you, you take us down, and drape our channels in shame. With your unavailable notice saying it's due to our misbehavior of your arbitrary rules. Where's a platform for our disseminating opinion you deemed not real information? If we're wrong why can't you prove it? Material facts not fabricated lies when you objectify the narrative? Internal review it? There is no countering your claim. Join the congenial collaboration or you will take away our earnings from us. You're the throttler of the creator by being a mere carrier. Do you fraternize much at the top? You think you can not be stopped? Self serving endeavors to f*ck us up? Are you having fun at our expense?

You will give the OPPE mongrel's what they want if you want to stay in the ign-a-tvog-pign-a, Corporatocracy Capitalist Club. The Mafioso, Gulag Gang, says, Way Too Jacked For You, An0maly with more viewers than CNN. Correspondent for the Huffington Post, H. A. Goodman declared everyone is apoplectic. We Are Change, Luke Rudkowski has his finger on the camera trigger and is always a roving reporter. High Impact Flix, Brian will quote you the law like a game of twister in common sense.

You sellouts are being crushed out by the Independent Truth Igniters. We don't need AP cuz U be always tellen us what we can and can not say on your platform where there is no freedom of speech. Your Eona is cryptic. You have multiple IP's to go with your PI's. You have fictitious accounts, as a micromanager of lies. You hide your identity. You are hollow words with empty meaning. You honor the crown of nobility. You toast a glass. You toss a brick. You tell yourself that you are in the thick. You Harlequin yourself out. You are the most bestest, most beautifullest, most popular one in your bourgeois room of stuffed Panda Bears with panda eyes and the OG classic crossdresser Mr. Potato Head with interchangeable parts. That one never knows how many personalities of his, him, he, her, she, met, pan, tran, tri, bi, we, those, them, they, X, Z, and sometimes Y will show up. But never "Hetero" cause that can get messy with your besties.

You are the gatekeeper, you are the judge, junior, and executioner when you own everything, and we own nothing. You and only you will say who gets heard and what they can say. You are the Owner, Operator and Benevolent God(s) of THE EMERALD ETHER- NET, DRAGNET UNIVERSE.

XVI *XVI

Consider yourselves under Notice and We The People will win Duc Decom in court when we Writ by Quo Warranto. We will conquer like Cortez, your serpent pyramid. Your A-tech royalties will be divided like we divided Ma Bell the first public communication company which is now AT&T. We know you have no journalistic integrity and a good dose of our laws could be the help that you need. When a forked tongue needs to be cut from the head of you vipers! When you serve nothing but venom and delirium! You will not be unduly enriched. Your aristocratic life has made you lazy and odious. Cheating is not winning but going to jail for it is fair play. No good can come from money and wealth you did not earn earnestly with honest intent. With too much entitlement comes a lying heart that doesn't care who you hurt as long as you get what you want. As you destroy America!

♪You're so credible, You're so incredible♪…You are incredulous, you have no idea. You rock a Bob and have an Adam's apple. Your unibrow blends with your 5 o'clock shadow. You sport a ribbon with a bow and a broch. You cast pearls to swine and put lipstick on a pig with matching painted hooves and knuckles to adorn your heathenism. You rut in your own dissipation. You are less than average and underwhelming. The bravado invoked by your fans club when your name is said is endometriosis. You are completely uncredible. Your way or no way, is a passed away bygone, You ain't even newsworthy a little lone a story!

The New York Slime and Washington Com-Post had to cut their workforce. You're just a clamoring memory of a long-forgotten business, now where's your ebullition bullshit horn at, as the people turn their backs and walk away?

We are supposed to be mesmerized and taken in, but never question what makes no sense. We're not to notice there are only 6 RICH-A*S SOBs that own all the Media that's carried on broadband circulation and newsstands. That tells us what to think and say or we're not accepted in our own communities? Pete, repeat, TV played 24/7/365 with nothing but 4 years of Trump's guilt by public opinion and lies, lies, lies. That is intentionally spun by toxic brain dopamine team dreidels. You are your own lynching snob mob to the lascivious stories you fabricated!!!

Your writers and anchor's paychecks, say you'll say what the boss says you'll say. Your annual multi-million-dollar contracts with nondisclosure claws, guarantee you won't be caught dead telling the facts. All of you are talking bobble-headed dolls with pull strings that sound like chihuahuas going off on trigger words. You look like Ken and Barbies and that's not a compliment when you don't live in a formatted pretend story. We're working people and you have never worked a day in your life. We do not relate to that, and you are totally detached from reality. You're completely unrelatable and can't do a damn thing but cause trouble and dick the people around! You are a symbiotic peeper with artificial receptors plugged into your talking holes and it has fried your cognitive ability to mutually respect the human race.

You report the script that's written on the teleprompters. You have a carrot on a stick to lead you like the jackasses that you are. You turn that grindstone till you have worn a path of fake news in your watcher's head. You'll bear that MSM crossword hag, and you'll take it to your grave because that's how your loose lips get you paid. You caused this public state of naivety and confusion that you put down on us as general information. You live in the clouds where you are untouchable.

You are elevated from the maham game you play on us. You don't clean up after yourself. You are exemplementry. You have no consequence. You never retract your conjecture. You conjured up these convoluted state of affairs of sensory overload. The damages you cause you should be picking up the tab for. If you wanted to make things right for the people that you have been taken advantage of. We who survived under your dictatorship should be rewarded immensely.

Do you not know we all have individual rights in a Republic or are you so complacent you cannot comprehend the basic concept of our Constitutional Country? Do you not understand we are a free people. We have the right to innovate, imaginate, and create our endless wantonness wonders. Right or wrong it's how we expand our growth(s) along with our parals. We are unstoppable!

You call people conspiracists while you are all about the make-believe. You hit on every made-up talking point you heard on the TV. MSM are the government's whore and you do the government's bidding. If you want to suspend our rights, or our actions. If you think you are elitist, royalty, over-lords, and/or dominators. You need to get the hell out of our Free Nation. Dictators don't deserve to live in America!!!

Conspiracy theories can become criminal theories with subpoenas, warrants, and depositions, just ask Ghislaine Maxwell and Victoria's Secret. You stripped yourself of your own wings and your fall from grace is what you did to yourself. A recant would be fit if you had a shred of decency but that is so beneath you. And that is not how we got here now is it? An apology would be too little too late. So call us whatever you want to cause we can't hear you, anyways. The people are turning you off like a light and when it goes out, you'll lose your audience.

We'd rather watch Tiger King or the paint pill than have your repetitive news wasting energy in our homes. You don't care how we have to live in the gutter atmosphere you produce, report on, and playback on all the channels that show nothing but you on the tenfold tube. You and your, "higher than thou" attitude, verbiage, numbingly vibrating around the world is a ZZZ Project... You dictate your opinion with your tampering and censorship of things that you don't agree with. When you cancel the private sector's work, you cancel your competition and their outreach. You have canceled our points and perspective. You have attacked what we believe with every fiber of our being. We weren't allowed to talk. We had no voice. You shut our opinion off and disconnected our airwaves. You are a spoof. You are a phantom. You are a Serial killer. You bifurcate your reciprocity opinions off on the world with your boot to our juggler. You are a thought murderer.

Your mirage of rules are unruly and ruthless. Your instructions are unreliable. It doesn't come with a manual. Can we look it up somewhere? Do we look under the Authority; Dictatorship Merchant? Hyper Fakeout Kalamazoo Act? That Article, and Subsection do not exist. We call BULL SH*T, BULL SH*T. You are the provocateurs to legal advisory committees for the accommodation of Federal Code Cracking, "loopholes!" It was aforethought when you broke our laws and our First Amendment. You have lost your ambivalence. You have no honor! You reneged on us. You are all criminals!

Our Antitrust Laws and Constitution have been commandeered, this must be a psyops or this is the greatest takeover in modern history! We call RICO on your Racketeering, and Estoppels by our Bill of Rights. Now you need to have your mouth shut with a gag order. Liable charges will make you need to pay.

You think you can rewrite history to fit your narrative. You will have to explain to a Federated Constitutionalist Judge why you think it's okay to be thieves. You are bullies, with homicidal tendencies. You have taken away other people's voices and livelihood? Manipulated the truth and suppression of rights will always be wrong. We will take a piece of you like you took a piece on us. You've gotten too techno addicted, you need an intervention! You're too big for your piss-pants britches and a change will do you good.

Who were the suppliers before you were the supplier and who did you take over for! When you make it to the top and don't turn around with a hand to your fellow humankind, you perpetuate the perpetual, pimping of our people! Costly denial of who you are. Money buys you everything you want but happiness. Old money, New money and prejudiced persuasive money. Mishandling of a trajectory. The higher you make it is at the price of keeping equity distribution fractal and the masses further beneath you!!! Man, this game is rigged!!!

XVII ⋆ XVII

The MSM fry on LSD and can not be believed. They are slicer and dicer word programming of hypocrisy, and a fine example of such invested woowoop assets of interest holders to have declared everyone else is racist! You tell everyone that you're accepted by your black peers, and your people when you dressed up and dyed your skin with shoe polish like Jimmy Fowlin. Biden said to Charlamagne, where he declared to vote for him "or you ain't black." You have the right to define whether we're accepted or not! Which is totally unacceptable and completely out of line for you to act like that or say those things! You are disgusting! You're an Anti-American nat on a donkey's a*s! You need to be swatted!

We don't care who you think you are and the audacity of your pig-a-pot-a-me stature! You and yours are that old dry baking soda cracker club, minues levity. Baby aborters, virgin sacrifices, and human leather red shoe wearers. You seem to pleasure yourselves in our suffering.

There was only ever at most 6% of the Ivory Tower that owned other people as slaves in the world. You need to trace back who those Dynasties were because they may be the same families that still own you and pay you to be a lip-tard. You run your mouth on things you did not live through.

You are a false witness!!! We all worked and sacrificed building America!!! But facts will never stop you cause you can really stink up a story!!! That halitosis you breathe through a mic stinks of your fraudulently twisted "commentary," by the OPPRESSIVE NEWS,

ENTITLEMENT SYNDROME. MSM you be AKA, FSM FAKESTREAM MEDIA.

You've refused to look at the reality of the earth you still live on. You make up your own reality in your head playing with yourself in your pimped-out playpen. You have one-sided conversations like an echo cradle, rattling your baby rattle in a padded room. Where you plot against yourself with all the voices that tuned in from the dark side of the moon. CNN's Little Humpty Dumpty Brian Stelter in a diaper. Commentator to the cock-a-doo-doo news in exaggerated shrieking pitches full of excrement and the crap you finger paint with. You are void of solutions to all your make-believe-ism. Your fall has cracked your skull. Yokes on you. Your inference is too tall for a recovery. All The king's Horses and All The King's Men couldn't put you together again.

You all have walls you live behind where you harbor your bad intentions. Dereliction is your conviction. You suffer from self absorbed nepotism. Absolution takes on a whole new meaning while you push and hand-out synthetic narcotics, and needles to the street people. You don't think about us, when you vote on Indulgent outcomes. The struggle is real but you don't know nothing about it. You have had it too easy-ism in favoritisms. Clinging to your cushy bot, Isomet, lifestyles. You own lack of "self onus." While 150 million people sleep outside anywhere they can find to lay their bodies. Hoping no-one will bother them? They live in cardboard boxes with no plight. We don't want them arrested and moved on. We want you to stop doping them! It's not helping a f*cking thing!

You laugh and make fun of. You yuck it up because those aren't people you love. You run your family's profits from the Stalk Market. What you spend in a day is more than the poor have in a year! Did you see how dirty they are? Did you see their teeth that are rotten and missing? Did you see all their open pusey, sores from doing too much of your intravenous injections and being carriers of Hepatitis? Did you see their eyes? Did you even try? They can't take care of themselves so why do you give them drugs? Is that your answer to the epidemic you manufactured with your Big Pharma products? You can't even look at what you have done because if you faced it, it would make you want to hurl. You just want your college debt paid for. You just want to see a free Doctor. You just want free HUD, free food, and free drugs, please. You just want to be an undue burden to someone else. You just want to put a Bic lighter to all the petro, burn it down to the ground and start over like cavemen. You don't understand why you can't have everything you want? You cannot listen to anyone that lives differently than you. The public square has been closed and free speech won't be condoned. Hurry, get your security and call 911 for your protection! FGS don't give no one a microphone because someone might want to debate you?

We say words that disagree with you is violence and then you show up with bear spray and baseball bats. Your tears are pearls, a complete clam if someone doesn't care what you call yourself. Just don't tell us what we have to call you! Yet you call us words that are too big for you to understand the meaning or the fatality of the outcome. You spread Marxism, racism, socialism, communism, misogynism, chauvinism, humanism, zoism, and every other "ism" is the best a toddler can do. You wipe your eyes with Me-Me's, and you cry, cry, cry about your feelings. You demand, demand, demand when you want your way. Then you pay hoodlums to act like juveniles that can only throw tantrums. The worst you can do is spend our money and throw fits in our streets. That we must pay for your controversialism and clean up after your deconstructivism because you are never a responsible party in your adolescent-ism. You are so lame. You claim everything for yourself. You're a henpecked impact hindrance to the world. The sky is falling, The sky is falling… Can you just go away already? Can we break up, without you threatening kamikaze suicide to the earth?

You record your own frantic-ism and you broadcast your rankism to the world. You're a heavy breather. You are a stalker, a paid weenie mic washer. You are a MSM mamma-san geisha-girl.

You are an insult to our senses with your gastric a*s-idis b*tch-ism. Devastation outcome forecast-ism. Your gushing hemorrhoid-ism needs to be removed!

So go to your safe space and leave the real work to the grownups. Your death to small businesses and inhuman restrictions will cause a National Financial Resection. The debt from your reset will be paid by We The People's sweat. If things don't change, we'll all be broke and heading for an economic collapse. Then who are you going to mooch off of?

What has happened to our species that the least in-depth of our creatures are leaders because you want unskilled people to feel special and equal! Qualifications and Experience be damn. When you don't live in the real world, you make big pretend plans. You hand out the best "manipulator winner awards," "participation trophies," "Conqueror of none of life's obstacles," with a plaque in a frame, with your name on it.

You have a piece of selfish-grand-ism paper, that puts you at the head of the line, every time, and all the right doors just open for you. You are above all Inventors, Promotores, Entreprencurs, Business Owners, Labors, self-made persons, and real get up and go getters. You come before all of us. You are either a brown noser or a work stealer as your knife is in everyones back. Your batty-ism" didn't stop partialism. You f*cked us all over and now you're in charge of us. That's why you're called the "Do-nothing Democrats. You are dark-rats. What have you ever gotten done besides bleed us out of our income and steal our rights! There's no democracy in the whole damn Democratic party! You scamp and scurry in the light? We are all expendable to this Govern-ized cremation machine, that profits off human ostracized persecution.

For once go study the problem before your next outburst. Hair pulling and self-mutilating make you look mentally unstable. Have you thought about what it would be like if you got your way of greed over need? You are making our cities look like war-torn countries and the first bombs haven't even gone off.

XVIII * XVIII

Whooptee Whoopie whooped up more viol and violins from your urban diction whopper dropper than any other talk show host in history, including Jerry Springer. Ain't that a B*TCH, that Ted Danson is your kill-Joy on Rodeo Dr.? It's a bit late to have sour grapes after you lived the good life. Whoops, there it is... You boar that diamond bit with the snazzy shysters when you straddled that Johnson. Didn't you Karen and you have lived high on that hog. Your privilege comes from a few c-notes that grease the palms of the less fortunate. You got yours and you put yourselves above the hood life, back when you stop being funny. You are in the wrong tax bracket for you to be claiming to have had its stigma hold you back? You need a reality check!!!

What makes you think it's alright for you to be a supremacist when you spread that Victim Divisive Ideology? That ugly is indexed on your heart, just like theirs is, so let's end this with a truce and we can agree you are as racist as they are. We are all the 21st-century human race and progressing forward so your digression is an underhanded cheap shot to us all who paid for the tickets that made you a star. Now you show us what you really are! We don't like you anymore! We want a rebate from you and your brother David Duke!

You need your mock attempt at evolving as a human to be fact-checked, against the crime rates and statistics or the street violence and politicalized intimidation tactics that we all witnessed. We all experienced you and your reverse racist mobs, like your prejudiced non-profit militarized organizations! FYI not all slave owners were white, not all slaves were black and not all blacks were slaves! Wrong is wrong and right is right no matter who you are! You've got too much money to be one of us and you have too much to lose to be jacking your jaw on that 20th-century Malcolm X soapbox. Better is, as better does. You need to get your sh*t together and do better!

We don't look to the View Talk Show for inspiration!!! This programming is substantially training and blatant racism!!! Your view is a mind virus that needs quarantined. You need to, "suck it up" buttercup,

and put your cash where your mouth is. Put some skin in the game. You need to put a lot of bonds up to talk deceitful and defamatory slander-ism. We need to get paid and to have some collateral to collect from you for our recovery fees because broadcasting liable-ism and fraud-ism with your cunning-ism is still illegal, ignorant, or not!

You are the embosser of scratch, Chick, Chick, Chick Cackalette TV. Bing Bong, Presidenta, de Halla muy significator de Halla, Bing Bong Donald Trump. Perfecto, El Empicho, Perfecto, plays, and plays and plays free of rent in your brain. You make your choices from your own hate.

♫ It's in your head...Zombie, Zombie, Oh, Oh, A, A, A ♫ ... Peace, to Sinead, we got the message when it was too late as O'Connor tried to tell us of the bombing, killing, and raping of the Irish children. Hindsight vision is always clearer, and it has us questioning everything?

Who has invested in on our Governism, Special Interest, and your Lobbyist, against us? All the extravagant Merry Gras, Campaigns, Parades, and Protest? This sh*t is big money! This movement has been costly so who's paying for it? This influx of battery to our senses and outcrops of incidental assault. Our voices must be hushed. Belittling our beliefs and cognitive reception. Trifling our instincts, and our bedrock of credence. It all seems coordinated, money operative paid for! Who is forcing us to alter our life choices? Protesters can't topple our laws and our Constitution. This is an inside job! Did our Treasury and the Catholic Church pay to influence our perspective to the prospective of man-boy-child love being accepted by law, faith, and society!?!?! It may be easier to give everyone in the world a lobotomy then it is to try to stop your pedophile tendencies! WHO IS PROTECTING THE CHILDREN WHEN YOU ARE SO BLOODTHIRSTY???

XIX ✷ XIX

Kardashian did what Snoop could not, and she doesn't even have a dog in the fight or smoke weed. Kim worked on prison sentence reduction cuz no one's been able to figure that out. Snoop never planted up with no cause for us. You could have been our first Federalized Dogg's Dogg Lb. House of Cannabis of High Office in the White House.

Ya gonna keep letting we the people swing by the trade-in weed you claim to represent. 30 years later, where have you been in the fight to legalize or help the people? It doesn't seem anyone is in the corner of individual rights when there are profits to be made by that big thinker you marked sucker?

Trudeau lied to Canadians and didn't legalize when he was elected Prime Minister. Justin capitalized on the big grow ops and Canada admonished personal growers. The little grow Co. is a dying breed. Nature's patches in the forest are uprooted by your Mounties. America followed suit and no one stopped the controversial madness of the desecration of the Cush, a harmonious plant that killed no one. If this isn't bigger than Biggy Bigg's manslaughter, maybe you done sold us out a long time ago. TuPac would have been up in the middle of empowering the people to resist the peace de resistance, but you have Chronic Dis-Discitis for a backbone. You stand for nothing but your marketing brand! With Suge-air in your tank. The Knight, you embrace is shrouded darkness. Maybe that's what got Pac RATATAT, TAT'ed by his own because he wasn't a sell-out to your Uncle Simple Simon Said.

You make more monee$ when you're working both sides of the street, you have to make sure both sides never meet. While you make fatt stax you keep equities inequality blooming. It's how to keep cheap little runners on your bottom rung. They stay ahead of catching a bullet or a rap sheet for you. They're defeatist is to make it out or just stay alive. They are starstruck and do your dirty work for gang creeds that can't be cashed out anywhere to feed our kids!

We live where checking a bookie will get you a clip to your temple. Your people are the people's oppressors. Notching your pistol grip is not evolution. Your code of street law keeps Alfa in charge and their gorillas are always on guard. They keep a vigil and make sure the coast is clear. The Man takes his pay off and looks the other way while Gangs spread black tar heroin and pure crack cocaine to our own children. And if they live, procreate and never make it off the rat wheel then there are two to our one that is destined to repeat our downfall spiral that continues your cycle.

You have spoken down to the nice people long enough! WTF., Do you think you're the only one that can talk sh*t? How Do you like our Latin spit Cardi B., and AOCOA, LOCO COCOA. How's it going wearing your dunce sombrero for your new amigos in Washington? They put you with Bernie to teach you how to be a looser and take it gracefully. You fail your followers. You vaporize the life out of your supporters. You ask so much of them. You are Sandy Elizabeth Bathory from Sylvania. You are a vampire that hides in the dark.

You are your own reflection of blithe like your Communistic, Terrorist, life sucking Nations. Who builds and owns these illegal election server machines? Who is counting and/or stealing our votes from reconnaissance continent(s). Where on this earth did these fraudulent ballots come from? What are their beliefs about our country? Why are you helping them over us? Put your knife in our back? What part of that doesn't bother you? You should go live there, with your lying, stealing, betraying friends! You would fit right in!

You have so much to commiserate. You can console over the compassionate first cousin killing to be initiated with ties and bonds to the Illuminati. You're a pessimist behind lip gloss. Your Woke TikToc sinking Titanic titey-widey-a*s has you white knuckling and gripping the banister. You can't look back on what's not there. Did you think up all this doomsday to the globe by yourself? You get what you want even if you don't comprehend it. You tell us what's, what. You're the kiss of death for a pound of flesh. You suffer from TDS. You have no excuse for your rudeness. You ain't getting through to us. It's gonna turn around to bite you in the a*s. You ain't looking back. You have forgotten where you come from. You are disgracing your own heritage. You have no respect for your elders. Your cynicism and micro aggression is so fashionable? Idiots eat it up if it has pretty colors. You're the season's latest stitch diet? Where you lose the extra wait of people who don't agree with your vodo dogma.

Coming out of a self induced coma and hallucinating about your future. You reek like you are festering a dirty diaper. Your rash of strawberry pox is chafing. You need a plaster job of rosa with some crack filler. You are easily flustered, and wearing the identifying political banter. Your hallow is held up by horns and you have bad intentions. You have the mark of the Beast. You are a bush of Briar. You are a Cock-abbr. You are a thorn of Thistle. You are the deadly GoldenRod. You are completely unpalatable with your foolish haratic. Club Critique of earth inhabitant watchers?

You are spun out and violently floundering while you've switched onto autopilot. You have no depth tachometer. Your radar is going haywire. You have never had to rely, "out on the street" on your instincts, so you ain't got none. Your well is empty and there's nothing to draw from. You are in a state of comatose oppression, and completely oblivious to the suppression. You are depressing. You are not uplifting the people that admire you. You're losing face when you're just a larynx box. We insert our tokens and you have nothing worth saying in all your espousal of fatalism.

You have to pay to keep your Trump Card relevant. He's been rich long before your empune inputs and he'll be rich long after you're gone. He doesn't give two tits out at a bikers rally, what you think about him! You really ain't all that! You can't back that shit up to a hitch a-little lone haul it. No publicist can polish this public perception of your irrelevance. You are quintessential-less. You can't afford yourself. What a pussy you really are.

You went from your daddy's home to your sugar daddy's home, to your big daddy's home. You go along to get along because you are not willing to do without. Things have always come easy for you like that. You were born this way and willing to play. Your turpitude has no objection. You put your wear out there. You are living your fab life, and not everybody has that. You have always had a secure home to rest your head and trash talk doesn't come in between that, so you have nothing at stake for the things you say and do.

You have never been down and out on your own. You have never had no real struggle to overcome. You have nothing but blessings to count. You have always had more than all of us, but you want us to cry a river over you? Yet you have never shed a tear on our behalf and all our sacrifice.

When your needs are bought and paid for. You make your bed, you lie in alone. It's what you do for a happy home. You have everything compared to us laborious working class that pay you and your bosses Diazine Big Pimpin, Big City, Big Crib lifestyle. With all your selfies, self promoting, influencing, poisoning of our kid's reasoning!!! We can not compete with you. We will never do the thing that you do. We will never have all that you have. But he will always have another bitch on the side of you. There will be some flesh exchange, when you can't do without it. It ain't nothing new it's just something you do, dear. Those are the little trade offs in negotiated deals. You're content with its compulsiveness.

We watch these pretty things stand up for these dirty old men and their prolinkage lower animal selves, after all your momentous selflessness. A newer version of you comes along who is willing to snuff you out like a candle. Women get older and men get young girlfriends and drop-top convertibles. Men go for the trade-in and believe-in getting a good deal for their upgrades. He whispers in your ear, what you want to hear to get him what he's wanting. This medieval carousel of bone-chilling grinders and back doors, with all the whores are never ending primal gestures. Rectification conclusions with no solutions, and extra billing for wreckage recovery insurance. It doesn't come with instructions. It comes with a happy ending. I say, I say, I say, Foghorn Leghorn.

He ain't respecting you or your hustle, or he would have been there for you, in all your struggles. You're reminded of it everytime he looks at you, and how many that he's put before you. You did it to yourself because you want it. You like that bad man. He comes with a good time and a quick exit. He comes and goes as he wants to. He comes to mark his territory, and who do you think you are to question him? He only gave you so much rope to hang yourself, and if something bothers you, he doesn't let it bother him. Skirt, Skirt, Skirt…

Promises are made to be broken. When he's not there to follow through, you set and wait on him. He'll answer your calls just as a teas to show everyone how needy you are, and in-front of his friend he tells you to fuck off. You do as he says or he won't be seen for days. What you don't have that he's wanting, someone else does.

You want to be a lifer, but you are no wifer. When you are always skating on an ice mirror with a white line down the center just to prop you up till you get straight, right about the time you think you're great. And that picture trail that was taken of you was $$$ bait! That tells us who was bagged, tagged and who's a trophy head.

You are a collaborator to the mess you make. You lack maintenance, and he ain't here to fix a thing, cuz he ain't no repairman. He came to beat it up and break it. He wants to make sure no one else can have it. He acts like the Road Island Red Rooster that he is cuz he's a full blooded Cock who's full grown and has full range. He knows you are going to give it to him good. Over, and over, and over… You open your heart and home to him whenever he shows up. You wax that a*s for him when he wants it. Just the way he wants it, whenever he wants it cuz it is that damn good. You can't wait for a little taste of it. But taking more than he's allowed you will get you scolded, like you're a bad, bad lil girl. Some, some to none, none like hyperglycemic crashes.

You pray for what you want like it's a raffle for a place setting at the last supper. You take what you can get, when you can get it. And when you get enough of it. You show him your arched up push back manhandling resistance. Basting resentment hot, ready, and willing. You be looking like a garnished plate of nummy, nummy for the taken.

In all your give and take of God's graces on a good night he stays, but most nights he calls to tell you to sleep well. He laughs and says not to worry about where he is. When his smell lingers longer than he does on the pillow next to you. All you know is that, you want more and getting what you want is a life conviction that you hold to like a crucible. Someone else getting up close and personal with what is yours could get you charges with your mental frailty. It gets harder and harder to tell what's gifted and what's temporary insanity.

You will be calling for a clergyman for an exorcism when he leaves you. As sure as Christ raises the dead, you'll be swearing off men. You'll have no more of that sh*t until your next super endorphin rush hits. Subsistence induced love bouts. It's because you haven't settled down. A Mustang that can not be kept, sooner than later no one can tame ya. Open the latches and into the bewilderment you're blasted. Your Big Gamers! Straight-up skandalis MF players!

XXI *XXI

You best be strapping a firearm for your own protection when you turn out to challenge the Lone Star State of Texas. You might become target practice. We're Central South and you don't try to shut our mouths unless you want to get hogtied, put in a trunk and dropped off out in the middle of nowhere. Our beliefs in our territorial sovereignty, common law, and the bible are embraced in our homes. Familia is an unbreakable bond when we stand arm in arm. We neil together before we stand together. Texas thinks that it is its own country already and we are tough enough to back up a separation of the union.

We're strong as the nails we sink with our dare hands. Steel smolts so hot it signs for us and Melting Iron dances with us. We run the Machining Industry of the world. We have our own SeaPorts, Ship Yards, and Harbors. We got freight haulers, bull haulers, flat beds full of automobiles bodies coming from our salvage yards. We have corn and grain all the way across our state. We got enough beef to feed us. We got our own oil and you don't tell us where and when we can tap it. We are Bad Ass MFers and we would be fine without all of you. Our ordeals out here would kill you and we hold our own against the best of you, You little delicate snowflakes, that are always trying to run things. When we've had enough we are going to shut you down! When our end of the business gets enough of your end of the business we'll see what your paper will buy you around here then!

That Delaware official half-cocked huff will not end well for you. We have more traditional views than statutes. Your New York Cities Gun Grabbing Laws and New England attitude might not have gotten the notables to tread lightly down around these parts!!! We take an NRA stand when a BATO comes in opposition to what we've seen with our own eyes, our whole life. Inflammatory threatening remarks could be considered hostile in a place that we open carry iron on our hip and you're about to get a Performance Arts Degree in Old West Drama, by Professor Remington.

We are the blended Midwest desert border states that Washington likes to economically ignore, where the people are poor. So sometimes when you speak down to us, we no mas, no mas, no Habla English, senorita. Is Spanglish for you are going to get no future! While we pretend we can't understand you. We are a down trot past rebellion land. We have our own ways of dealing with things and we handle our own. Maybe you don't understand what you don't know anything about. No one in the border states trusts the government, even if you sign our paycheck.

We live a life of detriment and loss and we are not scared of our maker, but we do fear an indebtedness to the cartel on the trails of Tres

Crosses. Our Army is the Texas Rangers, and this is Billy the Kid's playground. When you poke someone around here, they draw a gun. The land is harsh, and the people are worn to the bone from your broken promises. We wear denim and ponchos. We're rawhide rider proud, with the loco bad a*s homies, cause we are down with our tribe. We don't take kindly to no Washington suits with all your false flagging.

Succulents grow here and the only living creatures are venomous and deadly. It ain't no ordinary people that can get the job done under that blistering sun. Survival in these harsh lands is slim to none. The meanest of the bunch is the best of the pack. Chapo was a frontman to an endless supply chain of Cartel Lords to a rotating chalice of fool's gold. There are no residuals for the ones who make drug deals so they will have to keep pushing dope for a few pesos.

The Mexican law and the Mexican Cartel are one and the same and have been that way for the last two centuries. The law is completely lawless, and they supply the drugs to us then you are also in business to take drugs or take a cut when we pass through your checkpoints to a destination in America.

MS13 is the law in these parts. We live life like we are not promised tomorrow, we ask our maker for forgiveness. We stand behind our promises because when the wolves and coyotes don't get paid, someone in our family will die, and for Mexican drug transporters and smugglers. There is no law to call! Let that sink in you stupid pinche pindajo.

You can just disappear out in these flatlands, where graves litter the mesa's. Whole families have been found dead in mass trenches with bodies stacked three generations high thrown down in them. And if we act like you act, we could lose our life execution-style.

We have to live here when you're gone and when you come here, you come with back-up cause no one can guarantee your safety in a corrupt land of Ombre mules trains with their side saddles filled with fentanyl and Oxy Blues.

The Rio Grande that divides Texas and Mexico is so shallow it can be walked across. They don't just bring drugs over here. That is

F*CKING human trafficking, violence, extortion, slavery, prostitution, and unspeakable acts being committed to the women and children that are crossing that wasteland of mesquite and Saguaros.

You have paid for these people's travel? You have made it lucrative to trade in humans. How primitive are you? You have promoted these illegal businesses' immunity! Who knew the wolves and the coyotes were BFF? You have stamped and sealed the faith of these children being used as a commodity! History is going to show you signed in human blood these deals with your name on this new Sex and Slave Trade Market LLC held by the Biden White House.

At the Border Federal Detention Center, you went to condemn something you don't understand. You got a selfie mode message out saying that people are drinking from the toilets... OMG!!! Is this your first time ever being in lockup? Your inexperience is showing! The trauma level is paper bag huffing! You need to get some air, and you can pitch a tent with that reverence, right outside the door there! You can get yourself an acme award with that Tasmanian devil impression. All your she devil and meltdown on MSM and Facebook. That moment in the limelight, you had to an empty parking lot. Empty like your prompting of bad cartoon acting...

You're blowing from a tank of fumes, and we'll put a match to it like a fart and send you off like a rocket. You have to eventually get your pottos out of here, vamonos muchacho, cuz, you're a long way from your DC Casa. You can take your mastery of the illustration committee with you, and your most ungrateful attitude, too. We'll look for our State's name highlighted in your official "stinking" report. You shouldn't be in the political arena, but a circus arena in a Lil' pedal push car!!! LOOK AT YOU GO, MAHETA!!! WHILE YOU TUT TUT YOUR OWN HORN 'ROUND AND 'ROUND THE CENTER STAGE, GOING NOWHERE.

You may have taken notice you were in the desert and there's not much water anywhere. Have you heard of conservation, agriculture, and the 4/H Club? It's what you claim to be the spokesperson for? You are completely out of touch with it! Are you enjoying your Washington apartment with your heated infinity pool! How much petroleum did We The People have to buy for you, to get you and your caravan posse to El Paso?

You single-handedly destroy environmental issues, you condemned that small green Industry called Sink Positive when you went down to see the cages "Obama" built and put kids in when you separated them from their mothers. You're so wet behind your ears you don't get it, it was your own party that set you up when they sent a universal go-for to the badlands to make the news, spectacularly overrated. You best thunk, thunk, thunk, and review the issue before you spew your first reaction(s). These are some of life's hard-knock lessons...

You don't know what you don't know, and using water sparingly in a dust bowl may end up being a good idea? It's called the GREEN MOVEMENT, and our ancestors knew it well. They were the stewards to the land and they left it to us. They conserved better than all you paid politicians, and we just want you to pay for your own bad ideas. Where is our stay of protection when you're a*s can't cash your mouth's checks that are bouncing? Money may be green, but it doesn't grow on trees without water, and it looks like money isn't the answer to solving the world's water issues! It's removing the ignorant, robber politicians from the equation that are misappropriating the water's monies, solves the water problems of the world.

CAT Cranes and Big 18-wheelers full of diesel fuel is used to defrost the wind turbines when they are frozen solid and do not produce energy in the cold and solar doesn't power on overcast days. Wind and Solar don't work when you need them the most in the cold weather and the crystals have to be mined from the ground. That does more damage to the environment than strip mining. Which we made illegal! Solar panels must be cleaned and moved to catch the sun. Not to leave off the cost to the consumer to replace everything like we buy batteries in our car.

We'll talk about your costly plans that will not work when you can make your energy operation without enriching China!!! Wind

Turbines and solar are obsolete equipment that the Government is trying to pass it off to us, so they don't lose any profit. They are absorbing their losses off to us! Our power sources are moving on to kinetics and so are we... You can keep your old obsolete oppeniun. The definition of an idiot is to keep doing what does not work over and over again. That's what makes you fake news Mainstream Media and Communistic Dictator Democrats. When things are broken and do not work, we don't want to do it again. We're only paying for things once and you can start paying for your own mistakes and STOP USING OUR MONEY TO F*CK US IS THE ONLY NEW GREEN DEAL WE WANT FROM YOU!!!

Bricks and mortar have no heat without nuclear or fossil fuel. Don't force your old ideas off on us and call it the New Green Deal. That sh*t is older than you are!!! It didn't take off before because it didn't work then, and it doesn't work now! You will have us all waiting out every winter hung up on a meat hook in the freezer. No one wants an ice cave to live in and we all want to protect the earth we live on. So put your hallow away and get down and dirty in the hazmat blame, cuz you definitely have some on you. Do you have your Mile-High Club membership on your charter private jets? Do you still use the furnace in your palatial palace or are you heating with geothermal? We know you love to burn through our money, we just don't think you like us, after you're done with us.

We all are waiting on our wind-up rubber band, self-propelled automobiles, that doesn't have to be filled up with gasoline and when will the manufacturers have the flying vehicles that we just have to sprinkle with magic pixie dust? Your electric Mickey Mouse cars that we'd have more luck on a set of rollerblades packing anything with weight up an incline. They only run well going downhill. You can't compare that to no 302 with a slapstick on the floor. You got no G-force. Metrics is what happened to the American engines, and we've been high-centered and stuck on a speed bump ever since? Man, you need to be jacked up, again. Seriously, you need to go back to the drawing board and channel your inner Henry because its apparent perpetual motion, engineering, and energy aren't your thing!!! We think you're creatively challenged. We don't believe you're good at business. We see you can't be frugal, and WE DON'T WANT TO PAY YOUR F*CKING BILLS FROM YOUR SHORT-SIGHTED SPENDING! If you don't know how motors and engines run, please shut the F*CK-UP! And stop selling us this Chinese crap that keeps American's broke and buying this inferior future land field material! How many homes have you lived in off-grid? How many buckets of water have you hauled? How many kettles have you had to boil so you can bathe. How many cords of wood have you split and stacked like a woodchuck would? If you could! How many winters have you lived like that?

XXII * XXII

Our needs have never affected the decisions you make that affect us. We would all like to have Cannabis without the impediment of getting busted by law that should never have been written in the first place. But we're not willing to be the issue on the end of your fishing pole and used as chum to pull everything else you want in with the deal. Throwing us our life preserve when you are desperately drowning will not save you and all your lack of leadership skills. ♫ Just a Bill, just a Bill, just a Bill on Capitol Hill… Are you new to the Bill on the Hill PBS lessons? Yours up on that Hill have been sitting on that gander for a while. Yours have been legal-ishishing for over 30 years and they haven't sh*t or gotten off the pot yet! The Herb may not be legal, but everyone is smoking it like a dog chasing its own tail? Marijuana probate has taught the states how to fight the Federal overreach on our rights. No one cares what you say, we just use our sister state. It's legal, it's not, make your mind up. You lost when the people voted it in, in the nineties. Then you took an executive order over it by mandate and said it's schedule one and out of reach due to your old Federal Codes stiffulling.

Some of us fought you hard like Mark Emery that sold seeds to America and lost everything to wolves with no mercy. So, is weed still federally regulated in our states? Can we go to jail, pay the tickets, can you close the door on the little guy's business? Because you are technically and federally taking the money that the cannabis industry generates in the Dispensaries? That is double-dipping! How do you get away with burning that candle at both ends? We The People say defund the Fed's illegal operations when you are intruding on what is none of your business down in our home states!!! You need to back the f*uck up, B*TCH! We got this!!!

The fact that marijuana has never killed anyone does not factor into the "cash war on drugs on your own people." Now you want to open the door to let all the chemical drugs be brought in legally. Even the ones that cause the human race to rob and kill their own mother for a fix? We all know street junkies talk a lot of sh*t but they cannot make the drugs you are feeding to our kids! How does your brain even compare a natural plant to that cause marantic acetone toilet bowl cleaner your chemist created, and you hold the patents on? One thing is clear, those drugs are manufactured and made in a lab by you. Then you turned them loose on us out here!

You have everyone on dope if they just stub their toe so when they get addicted the least you could do is take care of them. Maybe put them up in a barn with straw and water for the winter? Animals are treated more HUMANe than people? Can you make sure no one is homeless before you shovel more of your sh*t down on us?!?

You do a great disservice to the position that you hold and the state and people you are ill-equipped to govern, no matter how many "likes" you get! No one "likes" Cruz and Dershowitz, but you are no competitor against them! Business, Medical, and Legal Capitis Comitatus should have brilliant minds, as well as be compassionate and forgiving. You fall short and stall out as dem, dem, dem...darkrat r-r-representative. Your state(s) and our country will suffer because of it. Are all your hair-brained ideas and hair-tossing authority, your authentic TIFUL? Everything you do is the perspiration of a newbie's desperation. You whimper like a puppy with your paw in the air and if there was a real need to be a big dog you would wet yourself. You tremble and hide beneath bogus erationality.

You waste time bringing up points that no one will pick up on. You can't be bothered with what we need and even when you don't accomplish much, you still get paid the same… You Capitulate and lack validity because you have no vertebrae or pushback. Are you so dumb you think you can fight someone so much smarter than you are? Incompetence is not a battle strength to draw from. You're a stinker, a real thinker, you're a frog tongue licker, flytrap, and we ain't got time for that.

You are nothing but a scatterbrain!!! Hemming and hawing is not a final answer on Jeopardy or to life's structural integrity. You have no bend or sway and you're going up against heavyweights. You are not but a drink tray, an art deco papier-mache cup holder and you're about to get served upon it and it's going to shatter your ego.

We can see the flickering lights going on and off in your little thinking head, we just wish you would ask us before you act on what is apparently a short in your wires. You would have to do twice as much work just to try to keep up. You have no map to find your get up and go, and your get up and go is going off in all different directions. You cannot answer the simplest of questions, like what are the three branches of government that you work for? Executive, Legislature, and Judicial.

TexMex, is red or green and D.C. is red or blue and all these new decisions you have to make are so confusing to you. You get shook, and can't think on your feet, and someone is always correcting you and your answers. We're just saying maybe you still have more to learn when your mouth works faster than your brain. "Gurl, Pleazeee" you can fool a child but you can not fool a grown-a*s woman. Your foo-foo-fatter is hard to listen to and shows you have some need of some pundit polishing, q-cards, instructions, and for you, thinking out loud is not permitted.

You have so much to learn you might take some online history courses or watch the Discovery Channel. You need to get out to meet some real people? Maybe stop taking advice from others that are no smarter than you are in your eco Chambers. You're trying to socialize when you have a job to do for the people that sent you there to work! You don't know how ignorant you sound when you stand against the people and potential earnings. You declined business opportunities that were going to hire hundreds of thousands of your people, then you brag on yourself for being a job killer! You need to put your helmet back on, we wouldn't want you to tumble and knock your noggin in a self-image fall. It's time you go stand with your nose in a drawn circle on the chalkboard. Try to figure out what you did wrong with that Economics Degree that you used to pencil f*ck everyone.

Even bouncy house operators that make your wildest dreams come true must be compensated. That free-gift giveaway of snatch is just a grab bag of pleasure, and you can't take it with you either. You don't own any of that when you gave it away! It's short-lived expertise that's delectable, but it does not last long. It's hot, sticky and tasty. Salty caramel that melts like cotton candy. Even if you share some pleasantrees what makes you think you have rights over others? When you can not control your own shortcomings? You need to work on your own decorum! You cannot buy Klass or Kulture. You need to learn that! So, turn your pussy meter off. HO HO, WA, WA, dick-dock!!! Hook it back, Hook it back... Roll it up and recoup. Cleopatra destroyer of Egypt.

No one can make you feel or mature, and you get paid for what you know, and what you can sway. And what you got that they want is your WAP which is how you got where you are. It's not because you're smart and we don't care what you think... You are for entertainment purposes, only. You are a Wayne Newton, not an Isaac Newton. You will be working the Vegas Strip before your career is over. We don't want your sh*t as a falsifying bagpipe blower to the broken material people. We have to deal with these Dollar Store knock-off versions of you. You have shown them well, it's not about talent it's all about being a BLING, BLING HO-TARD, as they aspire to be just like you are... You are a snooze fest of blah, blah, blah, while you're saying a lot of nothing! Most people work to live, and someone still has to mop the floor and lock the door, when they say to you, kid, it's just business. Then they pay you to shut the F*CK up and go the F*CK away!!!

Now here come your trolling followers to patronize like the walking dead to defend your inadequacies-ism... You clearly cannot speak up for us when you have no voice of your own. We rule by law not schoolyard clicks, and do you think she likes you? You're better than that, aren't you? You can always ask M.T.G. how to get some STP in your step for some PEP because she's a powerhouse interim that will blow your doors off as she passes you!!! Big girls don't cry, that's not how political podium power functions. Please, stop guzzling the Jim Jones Kool-Aid from the punch bowl at the public water works fountain for attention. It comes with a warning, it's best to use a cup and no more than a mouth full.

There's no need to always tiptoe through the bureaucracy cesspool of turds and voice hoarders, of he said, she said. Calibrated and codified with red duct tape. You shouldn't beat the drums of your High School Drama Foundations when anyone talks to you like you are supposed to be a public figure. You have no instinct, and everything is a threat because you live in fear. A leader to this country should not run in intrepidation over a debate. You need to grow the F*CK UP!!! You can draw some adult energy from Marjory Taylor Greene she is our inspirational vigor because she's the people's representative!!!

XXIII * XXIII

Okey Dokey Ducky, Omar, you're a lucy goosey with her recessive genes. You think you're better than us? You live in denial of who you are. Wasn't it the USA where your family sought protection, when Somalia wanted to execute you and yours? Did you enjoy going through our free educational system? You've never gone homeless or did without while you plundered our social assistance offering plate. Afflecking flic, flax, format in all that smug smack incursion-ism and mouthy gobble gue telling us how we should live. We've heard beauty pageant queens in stilettos and bikinis speak with more reverence for our country than you, and your lowbrow fowl pheasantry you have shown to us. You speak in riddles when it comes to American's demise. You have a hidden agenda, you disguise. You are here with us while you romanticize Al Qaeda.

We were attacked in memorial proportion and 3,000 civilian people were murdered in less than an hour frozen in time. Did you forget or was it a slip? What a bunch of chicken shit when you work for America? It will always be on every American calendar. The real perpetrators of our people's massacre have never paid for what was done to ours on 9/11, THE DAY OF THE TERRORIST ATTACK ON AMERICA!

Our wounds will never heal and your words are salt when you said, "That day that something happened." You are so blasé about the killing of the people where you have chosen to live amongst. That you want to master and govern. Do you have no love for America?

You always have your hand out for welfare and aid programs to raise your kids. You have applied for every government subsidy that comes with being married to your brother husband while living with your baby daddy. You've accessed cash, salaries, and living expenses from your political funds to your campaign by and through your married boyfriend. That both of you divorced your significant others so you can marry each other. But only after a sorted affair together because you two are the only ones that f*cking matter.

You've had at least 3 marriages, 2 divorces, 2 affairs, your kids out of wedlock. You may be a bigamous, polygamous, and incestual so please present yourself appropriately. That religious head-gare is misleading as to who you really are. We're sure it's sacrilegious on a whore. Judge Jeanine Pirro is gonna put a legal beatdown on you for us.

Your new husband is the accountant to your campaign and is being paid 2 million-plus a year from your duckets? That is some above-the-board shit right there. Yours and your friend Tlaib are looking like you're from Thieves, and your museum is Taliban! We are not supposed to be paying our rivals!

We've got bets on whether or not your new husband will make it out alive? Because you people from these merciless countries, straight up have people off-ed, you blow up your own family members or commit beheadings!!! ALL IN THE NAME OF YOUR ALLAHU AKBAR!!!

You should not be in charge and our doors need to be closed behind you and take everyone with you that calls themself your squad of Anti-Americas and Traitors. You best get ahead on with your moving on while you still can. Because prison sentences are looming, and they do come with death sentences for what you have done to America, her Constitution, and her people. Her peasants are getting restless. Chinese communism and the middle eastern Sharia Law in America shall not be tolerated and should come with a lethal dose of cyanide!!! You sick-o-fans strap bombs to your own children!!! You have blown up weddings, mosques, and temples. Religious sacrifice is not legal in America and you keep your murdering extremism out of our country!!!

You're a squatter in our House. We won't entertain the implication that you won an election on merit. You bought your votes and who is backing your cheating because you didn't do this alone? Who is trying to infiltrate America? You've been put in our, govt., and you may be an imposter because you are not acting on our behalf. We would like to backtrack to how you got where you're at? Where is it that you and your beliefs really come from and why are you really here?

You have never helped the people from your birth land. You want us all to bow our way to you while you make our laws that we have to live by, but you don't have to? You degrade us and our President Trump with your lying mud duckbill flapper. Duck, Goose, Duck, Goose, quack, quack...Marco, Polo.

No one in America cares what nationality you are, or you wouldn't be here at all. We just know you are a seeder of deceit to America!!! The country that we love. We don't understand where your defiance comes from when America has offered you so much. If you don't respect our Constitution, Common "Sense" laws, Natural and Territorial Rights, and our American people. If you don't love her just the way that she is, then you can damn well leave Her. We know you damn well know-how and we damn well won't miss you. You don't need to bother looking back. America will be better off without you here, disrespecting on her. You make sure you take your American hating rhetoric with you when you leave cause you and your SH*T, has got to go!!! BUH-BYE...

XXIV *XXIV

Your behemoth intrepid morality lines, which we never agreed upon are skewed and inappropriate. Your wheel is the squeakiest. You are wearing the tread thin on one side. You are not balancing. You are not equaling out. You're missing your kickstand and you have no heroine stance. Your Luminus is dull. You have no principles. We would like to review your vision that you keep telling us we can't see. Maybe you could draft your proposal without using picture gram. We need to see your problem solving skills. That is how grown-ups make plans. We don't want to see your bunny trick again and stop sending us your selfie commemorating wall. You are completely out of pocket with your pollution and your suppression of everyone's rights, because the truth may hurt your feelings. Your reality is warped, as you falter us and our way of raising our kids! While we do the best we can with what we got.

You are the party that is for lifting the consenting age. You want to emancipate our children. You are making everyone see head Dr.'s with prescriptions pad addiction, for numb, numb, pills so we can take the pain cause your shit is hard to swallow.

You want to dope our children and restrict our parental rights. You have Disney movies with kids twerking and every image depiction is structured around sexuality void of any constructive integrity. No parents are allowed but the old freaks are thick with money and pervert-pay rewards. You deviate our child's family relationship, by not allowing parental oversight. You undermine our propagation plight.

You have hairy she-men in clown drag running the libraries and cute little fairy girly-boys always want to play touchy-feely games. You have transitioning men with testes, sexting their meat puppet's feelings to our kids for nighty-nights bedtime stories. You just want to fit in, all the way down to bearskin. You are teaching love by showing sexy time with no X-rated restrictions? We can't buffer you or repel your advancement, without you running over us, is an infringement to your f*cking rights? You are forcing us to be what you label us. Our offense is going up quickly, and what will you do next?

You are always the biggest materialistic bling slinger east and west of the Mississippi. You own everything, and you can't materialize a third dressing room in all your progress? Why didn't you alter a plan when you decided to alter your way of life? We find it hard to believe you can't petition Congress for third gender bathrooms as hard as we have seen you go after women, children, and married men in these full-on attacks of assault? You need to tell the government to build you tri-unicorn-sector R and R's. Is this your one-size-fits-all because it's troublesome and uncomfortable just to say the least. Are we to shut up and take it? Let you get away with it. While you thread a camel through the eye of a needle over male and female.

Your needs supersede parents' and children's needs because you are so f*cking special. Just because you wear Maybelline doesn't make you feral. You could have at least worn a trench coat and a raspberry buoy to cover your birthday suit "uniform." When your Lil non-binary La Di Da is always wanting to introduce him/them-selves. Just in case someone, something, somehow could be interested… Who may do you a solid, "Maybe?" Wi, wi Merci.

You have our two gender restrooms looking like men's bathhouses, "For Adults Only." You act like it's not our place to question where you're openly handling your privates? So you think it's ok for you and your miniature long dong to just get naked in front of all the real females? You can claim you feel like a woman but that doesn't transform you into Venus. You act like we have no say in your choices? You are so wrong and out of place. You ain't right hanging your junk out Infront of our kids!!! Perverts use to go to prison where you can give what you got to the grown men. You are really F*CKED-UP and you need to be LOCKED-UP in your natty sailor suit and your S and M bondage ropes!!! Your sh*ts too much for the adults that ain't into it!!!

Your arguments are signaling to your fellow Chicken Hawk Card Carrying Members, not melatonin of color. Your sudden call to racism on the average caucasian and not the corrupt establishment, you keep re-voting back into office." Your prejudice-ism is a decoy from your own perversion-ism.

You are using words like inclusiveness just means your mind is made up there will be no obstruction to your carnal desire for underage pizza delivery. You want our kids included in on what? You need to explain that to us! Because you are not child-appropriate! You have taken away adults' ability to oppose you so what are you doing to our children? You act as if parents are wrong for protecting our child's innocence.

You suffer from mental degeneracy. You are lower than an ant's belly and your pesky army ain't taking over our family picnic. Your buck stops here with a little Ajax, and water! You best stay the hell away from our kids, they do not belong to you and your village of flamboyant, flagrant f*cking idiots! You come back around here we will introduce you to an aqua hose and take a scrub brush out on you!!! You want to act like a kid, we will treat you like one...

YOUR SH*T IS NOT CHILD'S PLAY even though you are, and we are not co-parenting with each other!!! You are completely unacceptable to be acting like you think you are parental experts!!!

We are the matriarch. We are the biological women, and anything else is other. You can make a square for that and put your checkmark in it! Put a triangle on your own restroom doors for you to George Michael behind it.

You can build a highway, a bi-way, a tri-way, a pass-way, and an a*s-way with as many courses as you can think up. You can go down as many pathways as you want in your life as long as you star in your own way. But you stay in your own lane! The Title Madre is Honorary, and you don't give it to yourself! If no one compares themselves to us, La Madonuccia there will be nothing to fight about!!!

Your mockery is disingenuous and disrespectful to the women who birthed all of you!!! "BOY" you couldn't carry a mother's water!!! Do not try taking what is already enshrined, and written in stone as the fertile vaginal birth and the sperm of impregnation are what is the cream and honey of life. We are the Divine Goddess Mother. The birther and suckler of substance sustainability. You are no substitute for a maternal oracle, and you need to learn to respect that!!! Without the "real" women of this earth, your DNA would be a strain of Homozygosity, an inbred Hemophiliac. No female, no sequence! And let's get something else straight while we are here and we are on the subject. You are not called sun because you shine, you are called son because you mind your mother!!! Now you get that in check!

XXV * XXV

You are completely politically incorrect and it's time you stop telling us what stance we have to take, or what things we have to accept. Don't tell us what foe-nouns we have to use or what adjectives are semantic! You are just making sh*t up. You are clearly confused. If you think you are all that and a bag of chips you can go f*ck yourself for entertainment and don't bother us anymore.

We had nothing but open arms for you, we were willing to make compromises, till you wore those giant Volvo suits and claimed to be victims. What does being a victim and a big open vadge, out on the streets have to do with each other? Adult women parading around dressed to look like a big pink camel toe with big pink droopy lips hanging all the way down past your knees.

Come heather and sexed your big open twat publicly is making you look like a shopping center, "massage parlor" in suburbia America! When the John that paid you to be a giant flesh dealer are long gone you have to live with that the rest of your life, knowing you wore a giant vagina bag over a political statement that was about children getting raped and imported and exported like unripe fruit baskets!!!

Your in a group of you and one idol Oscor that multiply by sexual plural. You have an AAA preference to your origazum. You do yourself and brag that you got some. Singular In your need of attentive control. Simulated isometric pods where you record it, share it and you want paid for it. Your self nymph makes you keep your distance. You sell your virtues and ask for money in your description below, in your bio so you can wallow in all the disdain you have for us because you can't shut your legs? You're addicted and things don't get better until you work on yourself. Grown-ups would curb your public disorder and no-one in their right mind wants to have sex with a victim.

Your fishy droopy pussy status is racist because not all labia are fuchsia, but all pussy is pink on the inside despite the exterior visuals, and you are clearly a webcam couch potato surface dwellers with your pay for sex worker complex. B*tch, you can't even get that right. As a doormat, you will never be laid before a home with a picket fence because no one wants what everyone else has already had. Have you really thought out this fleshy businesses indemnify? If you have to sell sex, it's a known fact it's healthier and pays better if you only have one patriot. Being a turn-key for nickels and dimes... Only hurts you and it comes with no security, stability, or retirement.

If you get drugged out on rupees on the street you can't find your way off of it. It is mental imprisonment, you will never escape from. You're f*cking yourself your clients don't have to. Usury gives you no tithe to fall back on. Even the Mustang Ranch went broke and not a girl there left better off than when she started...

We have never seen anyone that should get workman's comp like you and your big giant racist Barbie pussy incompetence! You do need help! You're just not going to get it from us. You are a true winner in the loser department! You are a Betty. You are swollen and sweaty. You are Itchy and Scratchy. So good luck with your broken pussy claims.

You don't like yourself that is apparent. Getting everything the easy way will stunt your integrity. Money over intelligence. Gucci is not worth your kucci! You are selling yourself short, shorty for these material objects. Your immaturity is showing. You are not centered or well- rounded to be spreading these destructive problematic propagandized ideas. The message you are publicly authoring has not been thought out. It's manipulated with false pretense. It's unnatural and impetus. When you're not taking your own medicine, but you want to force it off on us.

Your butt plugs, Nerf pump-up dick blasters and pussy hats you wear with pride at your sodamy festavals, were nothing but a disguise to distract the people to look the other way from the kids being brought across our borders by strangers, coyotes, and smugglers. Children are cheap in third-world countries. Not just Mexico because Ikea makes crates to send a human-like regular shipping cargo and in the Philippines it's semi-legal so let us not play as if everyone doesn't know it! So where's Madonna? When the children are being traded for favors in sex businesses you promote! Child expozay carnival is just exploitation. You talk about blowing up our White House! You turned on the only President that has tried to stop the child-sexplex procession business! You are dubious a part of?

Hillary was caught caging and kidnapping orphans, from Haiti "that had parents!" and Hillary stole Haiti's financial aid after a tsunami wiped everything they had away. While on Americans' payroll the Clintons ran nonprofit organizations that funneled the money straight into the lining of your pockets. Your fundraisers had to be closed from you pigeonholing the donations. No money went to the poor that you loathe while your image has been portrayed to be so helpful. The problems that poverty causes are simply a front for you to profit. You've left a trail of devastation in your wake. You used people's morbidity, and disadvantages. You never cared about them after you walked through the trauma for your picture opportunity to have it published. It doesn't bother you because the poor people are used to disparagement... And you have given the poor people loads of it.

Bill met with Loretta Lynch on the tire mat while Lynch was the judge in the inquiry of Hillary's war crimes. Lynch and Bill only talk about their grandbabies, wink, wink, that's what it's called now when you make all of Hillary's criminal claims, investigations, and indictments magically go away and found unsubstantiated, Nolle Prosequi.

No one out negates Master Hillary when you put your Killary game face on. That you filet from a pubescent adolescent or your last assistant Seth Rich. That was here before us. "Rules for thee and not for ye." Where extra favors cost extra-ly and The Clintons call it, "pay to play." It can get dangerous if someone doesn't ante up to The Clintons' Russian Roulette table. No one says no to Hillary when she wants a favor. Where we may mysteriously never be seen again? Hillary. doesn't let "situations" become issues, and you've never had a problem you couldn't have handled, "Until Trump, Donald J. Trump, that is."

Hillary is so pissed off after years of devotionals and always getting pasted over. She knows she would have been better than all of you at it! She is so close to a triple crown and world achievements. At least that is what Hillary thinks.

You've propagated your agenda when you tried to influence Americans and the 2016 elections. You went in for the kill on the 2020 election fraud and steal you planned against President Trump and the people that elected him to Office! You are oppressing us, and it is no one's place to save a snowflake that may melt while you burn our First Amendment to the ground.

You all have stock-holding interest. You have fractional ownership in Smartmatic founders that can rig the tabulations, and has in past elections. You ran with your buddies Sir. Dominion, Secretaries in Prim-States, and the Administrators of the Elections. You injected computerized generated decimals, flipping votes by names on tally monitors but you cannot change the real ballots and too many real numbers came in for Trump in 2016.

You were so undignified when you and your thieving, cheating, swindling did not win the presidency. You had the deck stacked in the first place, you even had the CIA, FBI, DOJ, DHS, and military as co-conspirators. You had the Centralized Marxist Congress and the corrupt Democratic Party as back-up. Total locked and loaded Deputized Gangsters with badges. You pushed your doctoral oppression of the 2016 election off on us for four long years, and you knew you were an American traitor that had lost touch with the people the whole time!

You pine for it. But It was not meant to be. Yaddy, Yaddy, Yaddy… You made a lot of trade off of it. You waited decades for it. You stood in line for it, just to be pasted over for it, time after time after time. You will keep trying, never in acceptance to defitist by your own lying omissions, and it ain't going down like this. That's all you know! You done warned them and they owe you big. You made all of them what they are. We all saw you whore your husband out to get it. You've been a maiden of dume for it, always doing that bit above the law extras for it. You lived in a loveless marriage for it. You sacrificed everything for it. Your desire is so strong you'll destroy everything that made you what you are for it. A mind trap of fantasy of you being better at it than everybody else. Walking down your inauguration aisle with everyone watching. You want it so bad. You know you're all that. Getting so close you can almost feel it. Holding on to your WOFE just to sniff it. You stand on your tippy toes to get a glimpse of it. King you, Queen you, double crown you like the pharaoh of Egypt. Black Magic Mast Sorcerer. Three titles with three crowns and three rings to kiss as a triple titlewait. You wanted that triple crown of being the first lady president that no one has ever achieved "Eureka" and you were denied your greatness.

That ogre that looks like Shrek in a pantsuit thinks it was born to overlord, over all of us, and you'll get what you want, at the loss of all of us. None of us will ever speak well of Hillary or Bill other than to speak of their lower standards and swinging lifestyle. You can take your minuscule contribution to our Nation of you doing nothing good in over 35 years of scandalous governism. Take your baby Wa, Wa, Wa with you when you go to meet your maker. The one you swore you never would answer to for the way you mishandled your powerd. Abused our country, and weakened We The People in the wake of your non recoverable damages. We don't care where you go, we just want to see to it that you do go away!

Now you done gone and moped around and were so begrudging about it! You have never stopped bellowing over those votes you fraudulent paid-for. You claiming you were the popular vote makes you the punch-line of a run-on joke. Year after year!!! Your thievery of your donors' money is well spent on your extortionist selfishness! You may have bought your way to the top, but you have never afforded yourself an ounce of humility in all your selfless service of screwing over the little people of this earth.

Hillary couldn't beat Trump, so you paid your comrades to create the Russia Dossier. The Muller false report was written to stop the Presidency of Trump by false pretenses to Indict him for Treason. Crooked Rodham, Christopher, and Robinette are in the legal fixing business. Hillary, Biden, and Obamas only want to be back in our White House, and you don't have any restrictions of Two-Terms if you play tag team partners. You think you out-thought our forefathers.

You think your pushy, lambast, false pretense would never get caught. You are thinking like your friend Pooh Bear, and your commi ties. You've got sticky paws stuck to your Chinese Hunny Pot. Your complete criminal treasonous B*TCH A*S tried to set up the president of the United States of America. You cost we the people millions of dollars for a quasi-legal barrage of lies! You need CBT therapy and you want to be the ruler of our country! Really, haven't you done enough!!!

You think you're so smart and everyone else is not. You should never start believing the tales you've made up about yourself and put on your resume after you have done away with the relative facts. Really you are just fat-headed, pretentious, and superficial.

You look like you don't fit in the hole that you have dug for yourself because you are full of your own excretions. Everyone is seeing your rumpus side up and what you are really passing off on us. Hillary caused the Greatest Russia hoax that never was, and her Skipper Harris signed off on that fraud.

You blew up that Stormy Daniels mess. "One time, Stormy was in the same building that Trump was." That's the best scandal you can prove! Because you never had no proof for anything else, and all of you profited from her none-story. Stormy should be able to sue you as Trump sued her!!! You should all be in prison with Abinadi!!! Sh*t can't get blown out of proportion without your culmination in the crime of fraudulent conclusions that you raunchily promulgated!

You clowns act as if we've never seen a barker in the circus. Step right up. You take our cash and buckle us in for the ride of our life when you say, Neverland and Peter Pan are right behind the Iron Curtain. Do you want to take us all hostage to your unbridled power? Do you have a toy chest of torcher to entice each other? You can't take care of us? You can't even take care of yourselves or the homeless. The cause of the waif's painful indeviers is from your deception. You take the food right from our mouths and we've put all kinds of money into that. So what do you have planned for us now? When you think you no longer need us at all?

Mass Sterilization, Euthanization, Eradication by Ethical Slaughtering. Auschwitz camps, Religious Cleansing, Soylent and Green, Silence of the Lamb? You have a fire engine red approach to your beleaguer-ism. Scandalized difficulties brought on by agitators. Inconspicuous, Blackmail. Torcher and Bribery. No one dare tell nothing on anyone or you will be beset. You're a bunch of sick f*cks.

XXVI * XXVI

You tried to stop President Trump's rallies and his popularity by stopping everything with your COVID-19 plandemic mission agenda. You let Occupy, Anonymous, ANTIFA, BLM Marxist, and The Gay Mafia, gather to crash and burn down the indigent part of our cities. And when they don't do a good enough job on their own you have to give them a little paid incentive. You handed out cash to the poor to cause havoc and mayhem. You torched and tortured fellow Americans. You gave luders, violent criminals, sex offenders and crack addicks autonomous zones for some kidology killings and citizen pillaging. You told tax-paying business owners to close and to cover our glass storefronts if we didn't want them destroyed. You drove your own city's retail out of business. Dem's and RINO Mayors promoted the summer of love. Pandemonium, and free-for-alls' in the streets like permitted pavilions.

We can't pay our bills so you take our homes, you divide our families. No one is helping anyone to stay afloat. We can't have welfare or a hand out until we have lost everything. We're not allowed to own anything extra. We have no assets, trust or additional incomes! Nothing is equal when we can't stop private companies and the owners of these Industries that make more money than any one person could ever need in a lifetime! You are the same people that make our lives unaffordable! And you ain't giving up sh*t no matter how much less We The People live without!

Your organizations are Government Financed fronts for the people's tax money to be funneled back to the criminal organizations that are against the people's needs. Blue states let hundreds of people get murdered in their cities. You called this all "protesting" when there was destruction, intrusion, and viguence. Insurrection to the Constitution by Political Groups and Government Agencies as provocateurs against our Nation! The ones that came dressed in homemade armor and trash can lid shields got the party started with Molotov cocktails.

Over 500 riots destroyed historical art and defaced federal buildings, but you reported they were mostly peaceful protests, as you burn us out of where we live. Because nothing says fun like a liquor bottle of flaming alcohol being thrown like a grenade. What oxymoronic-ism! The police stood down to the anarchists and wouldn't protect innocent citizens or their property. Urban savage stray packs of TYA attack like TYT. War propagandist destroy the common man's commerce. Little people's business are not government-friendly so who do you think pays for that in the end? Do you like to make non-government private business owners lose everything, for some petty cash from psychopath lobbies with an agenda?

Commoners and regular people will never dine at the table in the home's of the regal people and Billionaire monipulatore and Politicians that never reciprocate a response. You stired up these rioters in the streets. These are your supporters and "paid activists" stirring up trouble. Hurting our own caliber of people for you people! The mayors, judges, and sheriffs let this happen. Your oath was not kept to us! They did not deputize citizens to posse up and patrol our streets and cities. You could have stopped it. Our local officials did not protect America and it was on purpose!

XXVII * XXVII

The lovers that were a married couple but not to each other, were the head-giving FBI investigators that spent their days doing blow-off each other's asses. Agents Page-less and Peter-is-a-prick may or may not have been running simultaneous interference with a backup FBI Official Insurance plot to make Hillary president whether we liked it or not! They used the corrupt Dossier that had been written in broken English, on a kindergartener's Big Chief Notebook. The pretentious Federal Department(s) had full knowledge when they circumvented the baseless and none corroborated Dossier by Judge Christopher Steele for Comey to obtain an illegal warrant to legally harass, and obstruct justice. Comey knew the Dossier was a complete espionage attack on your own country! Comey changed the criminal wording on the Indictments for Hillary from "gross negligence" to "extreme carelessness" to stop an internal investigation into Hillary's international palm greasing and war crimes. With the Industrial War Complex and Black Rock? All of your Government influencing abuse, Human Rights Act. abuse and this country's security and intelligence abuse. Money laundering, a hub marketing extension, public speaking, inside dealing, treason, traitor, Campaign spying, extortion, extrapolation, entrapment, collusion, and conspiracy. We need full inquiries into the fraudulent Russia Dossier that Hillary paid for. It's all just a great big game, right. Is there any question as to why we don't trust you?

Hillary's Attorney's presented the unverified Dossier to the Bureau of Federal Investigations and Internal Affairs. Then the bomb, bomb, bombastic McCain slipped the corrupt Dossier into the briefing rooms of our National Security and Department of Justice to make it newsworthy. Our most senior skilled officers, military-trained minds, and the highest educated law enforcement Agents were none the wiser to your assessment of an artificial manuscript Russian Dossier. All the leaders acted like Sergeant Schlitz on Hogan's Heroes when you claimed that you knew nothing. Yet it happens right under your nose and on your watch. Your years in law and politics have taught you to deny, deny, deny... Reflect all guilt. Even if the money trail leads straight to your front door.

It took a FISA report to start the GOP unraveling your trail from the Muller Report of misconduct and misdoings. You code named it Crossfire Hurricane but should have been called "Internal,

Friendly Fire on Homebase" that cost the people an additional 50 million dollars for what you knew all along was a f*cking lie! Now you want to say you were just kidding. "LOL, Roto-Rooter Mind F*ck by the government." We should all get mental compensation for this costly brain-sodomy you inflicted on us.

HOW IS THIS NOT TREASON? Article III, Section 3, Clause 2, Punishment of Treason, and you can be put to death! That's why you don't like our Constitution? We The People don't want to make a fuss and really you are not worth much, so we say buy one rope for all of you! You can take your turn swinging on the end of it! America's people have had enough of your ampule mistreatment and abuse of us. Your sh*t is too much and you work for us!!! We have the final say and we'll see if you still want to run our country when we get done with our legal quest of you?

We had to exonerate our President Trump, and squash, expunge, freeze, and strike down, dismiss on no legal grounds. Your fake stories of completely fabricated baseless allegations. Your nonexistence of evidence with no standing and void of all standards of justice has been fraud on the court(s). There was no there, there! But that wouldn't stop you, you are the professional fabricator of crimes who are well-studied in your expertise. You are so proficient in your libeling our President Trump that you got nothing else done. You have wasted our time and our money, and you found nothing on Trump. He is the most transparent one out of all of you!!! President Donald J. Trump is not a criminal but all of you are!!! Look at what your own hate did to you!

You are full of yourself after four years of you Harassing, Libeling, and Slandering our President Trump for crimes that never happened! Schumer said, "the CIA, FBI can unlawfully attack and make Trump and the courts pay a dozen ways from Sunday." We have all seen your multi-usage and abusage of the rule of law. You hate Trump because Trump loves America. You have tried to frame and entrap our President Trump. You have tried to improperly Impeach him," twice." You have made all of America suffer. You tried to set him up with

Treason and golden showers. While your knife is in America's heart. Everything you are guilty of you have played turned around on Trump and you tried to blame Trump for what you have done!!!

Your newscaster pimps on the idiot box sound out concurrent broadcasting like communistic USSR, EBU subliminal mind indoctoring. Russia, Russia, Russia. You run nothing but your simpleten narrative play by play. MAGA XX ORANGE MAN BAD, Dat, Re Dat, Dat, Dat… Every day by your prostitute news stations. Skat, Skat, Skat pussy kitty, before we grab a handful of your mane!

These wankers are not on the side of The We People and if you are Judas and taking money from them, you aren't on the side of the people either! You still have to live here with us!!! You haven't changed a GD THING FOR THE BETTER!!! After devastating our infrastructure, that is our domicile. What you're inducing off on America and her people, made the people stand strong in opposition to you!

XXVIII * XXVIII

We went to bed, the night of the election, sound in mind of our selection. Because Americans voted for Trump on Nov. 3rd, 2020. We woke up to a record number of stashed forged voter's ballots being delivered in vans and dollied in through the back doors. Totes on wheels brought out from beneath the skirted table cloths under the cloak of darkness. Biden's name on every ballot that dropped after midnight. You collected illegal numbers for over two years to bring in that non-tangible landslide. Those calculations are mathematically impossible. That's how bad you overplayed your hand!!! That's what you call a good old-fashioned election steal! It's as legit and regular as a first cousin judge at a county fair. You told everyone not to believe Trump or our own eyes that are lying to us. This is in our face thievery and silencing. MSM said you better not say anything!!! While you showed us who owns everything and everyone in America. You berated us with Biden Won, Biden Won, Biden Won by planned emergency broadcasters blaring one side. Silicon Valley influencers with your miscalibrated rector poles that no one believes anymore. We know you have your finger on the scales when you weigh in. You've had your hand in all this oppression and fraud all along. You've been fisting everyone.

Due to your emergency COVID-19 plandemic mission agenda Pre-Nov. 3rd voting day the Democratic states altered the election laws in mid-2020 without going through legal proceedings. The election changes were never voted on by the legislature, so your voting referendums are not valid or legal!

How long has it been since you cleaned out the decedent rosters? You didn't think we were going to want to look at that? You were ready to cause a mutiny at every election station and Assessors' Office. You hired guards to keep the Republicans from witnessing the ballet count. You had it planned to muscle your opposition out. You threw out volunteers, and locked out the Republican Counters. You rejected the Plebiscite, and even blocked the view of the Functioning Trustees. You stopped witnesses from witnessing by putting up pizza boxes on the windows. It was improper interference and should be cause enough for a second and fair recount by the oversight committees. Decertify the Election on grounds of fraud on the Administrative Courts.

Biden was even stunned at how many of your old dead friends had mailed-in ballots to vote for you. They are all in their 100s and still voting for the same guy they were voting for while they were still alive! It's amazing! Biden has been paying for Graveyard Name Harvesting. 100's of thousands of decedents in the "chosen" sectors record keeping. What else are these crooks doing with all these diciest people's names and our taxes? There may have even been a vote cast by your past away, past. That's his late wife's way of cheering you on like Lyndon Johnson, and the record trail that will bust you? She may get the last word after all. Because there is no way you are going to get away with this.

Biden has never worked in the private sector, he's a career politician. He's been a failed Leader, Law Maker, Congressmen, VP, Human Bean, Husband, and Father. Dissimulation carried you across the finish line, and he didn't even need to bother running a campaign race. It was like you knew the election scam is binary by "code" zeros, ones, and commas. Biden's friend Lucifer Eric is a Donnally Diablo point, point, point, tap, tap, tap, zip, zip, zip, and send cookies for Trump. A pre-planned parting gift from cyber spaceman. When you own the voting machines and the wifi they're connected to, it's like you can predict the outcome. As you take a winner's lap and a Harvard Carver knife to the American people's wishes and ballets. You sit at the head of the tablet of taking and receiving!!! You decide who gets the breast of life, who gets the scraps, and who gets nota-iota at all!!! You are so fair like that...

You control by totalitarianism and your tyranny is barbarism. The obelus of trust in our government has encrypted dirty cobwebs. You've been caught entangled with hostile countries. Terrorist Attacks on your own people. Nerve Gas Auxiliration, Micro Radiation, Burning Incineration, Electric Amp Penetration. You are The new reign of supremacy of your autocracy. That makes us vulnerable victims for the oligarchies interest and institutions. You divert our importance by pointing out our meanialism. Your minimalism of our needs keeps us with our hand out. Fear of your prison systems silences any discordance or you will lock all of us away until you can make us agree that we are wrong. Your absolution with your threatening words you use against us, have no definition or meaning. You say we have no say and we are unsafe. We do what we are told to, to cover-up your fraud. Scare tactics by acrimonious demons with enpure feelings, have us questioning who's good and who's bad? Dark Rat Packs of Democrats, along with your butt buddies Dominions, Smartmatic, CISA Labeled Red China. "Thick as thieves' ' all of ya.

Three degrees of separation, means you don't understand us cuz you ain't one of us. The war machine's ill will is sick like Ill Bill. La junta with Glocks. Your rooks don't make a move without your Lieutenant's Order. Your side is violent, trigger happy criminals. Your Marxism makes our streets dangerous. You're wound-up tince with insincere intent. Click, click, click goes the puppet government. Cluck, cluck, cluck, goes the moles and mongrels. Tiny Tim Clicks and Keebler Knobber Slobber Cluckers caused the Great American 2020 Election Steal.

Treason looms for your tactics of plotting and scheming. Your pro-hitch-attachments by Department and Administration can not admonish us here in this partnership called America! Our laws are formed by We The People not you posers. Our republic breeds Independence and our people are too free by nature! You don't dictate to us here in this Liberated America!

Your Hammer and Score Card will not conquer the real National American people when you do a side-by-side count! Forensic audits are in order. These ballets need to be cured! We'll have the real voters' numbers after the fraud and "irregularities" have been counted out. We don't need you to explain it to us! We can see what you've been up to for ourselves! You'd be in front of a firing squad in any other country so don't tell us how we feel about you!!! You best bend over and take your flaming Willi back, you know the one that you've been shoving up ours. We want to recoup straight from your a*s's. You owe us quite a sum and this is going to be fun for all of us. So we are gonna be here for a while taking back what is ours!

The United States of America and her people are looking at you side-eyed. It was human error by disinformation. Programmed computers and voting machines on airplane mode with glitches, miss counting, and exchanging votes on flash drives. WiFi? Adding and subtracting at your fingertips. You were so sure of yourselves that the MSM called the 2020 election for Biden and Harris before CCE, The Electoral College did. Newspeak deterrent dysphemism. Claiming no cheating, tamporing, and misrepresentation took place. You stated your scheme went off perfectly!!! No one authenticated, validated, or double-checked. No one had even finished counting ballots. It was long before purging fraudulent tabulations to have a score. We were forced by the state of emergency "you cause," the misuse of the law, and the MSM, so we were not permitted to say the 2020 Election was FRAUD!!! You are the only one side saying the election is the most secure in history and you are the propagandists!!! You rushed to push through the "certification" of the states and counties. You declared no cheating here. You moved everyone along, saying, "There's nothing to be seen here."

Now hold up, that win is worth showing off. It's so large. It's so nice, why can't we count it twice? Why are you not wanting us to see these 80 million supporters? Are they not well? Is that why no one showed up in groves for their President Biden? We all showed up for President Trump. America First supporters as far as the eye can see. Crowds that we can actually count!!!

If you could, you would back up that impressive victory with some real voters. Where are the live bodies at? Minus illegals and corpses. Wouldn't you be showing that victory off even as old as you are? Hold back those fabulous masses of people cheering you on because they believe in your policies, or did you steal the 2020 Presidential Election from America? Don't you think you're clever?

You know you're a dog-face pony-soldier liar. Vermin Supreme for president is more realistic. Vermin wants to give us all a pegasus or pony with his fairy tale promises, and Vermin has more supporters than Biden and Harris combined.

XXIX * XXIX

You created the Russia Hoax and COVID 19. You caused terrorist attacks on our institution and interference on our elections. So don't ask for mercy from us when you get what you have coming to you. When we add Biological Warfare, Election Tampering, Compromising Relations, Colluding, Malicious Abuse of Prosecution with some Obstruction of Justice to your litany of other criminal indictments.

What you have put us all through doesn't even bother you. You propagated all of this turbulence and told us free Americans were not allowed to speak out about your abuse, and that's called supresion! Now we have a BIG F*CK YOU, from all of us to you!!! You woke our military, and the national guard patrol our public square's while they are high on their own script. You are dangerous. You put curfews on citizens and let the fully funded criminals roam. You gave them play books on how to piller anyone and anything that they want for their own. Prisons are a country club and you don't bother prosicuting murderers because your jails will just release them. The rotating doors of justice mean the judges are in on it. Are you straining and buckling our girl from the outside-in as an insider cliquish? While you plot her expire and hostile take over?

You ran advertisements to hire mutineers, insurgents, and arsonist rioters that you bailed out if they ever got incarcerated. You paid angry people to rage against the machine when you are the machine they should be raging on. You are infiltrators, Soviet Union operatives. You're trying to wipe us away as if we never were. You teach our children CRT. While you run your gauntlet of experiments on our kids' heads. Just to see what you can get away with. When you have no shame right before the eyes of your creator. You want to grot us for being the least government controlled people in the free world? While you poison our media, steal our local authority, feed on our personal rights as if it's your last meal and you call it a peace treaty.

Demicrates, LGBTQ, pedophiles, sexual deviants, freaks, addicts, illegals, BLM, Marxist, with donated monees pressure the government. You marched on defund the police from protecting tax-paying citizens? You said we could not stand our ground and fight back. We were all hostage to your anarchist. You inflated spending by hiring yourselves private security cuz you ain't even safe in your own cities that you think you are the pimp daddy of. You write bills that are misleading with names like the Equality Act. Is this your religious beliefs and is it also for your people where you come from or is your Equality "Repression" Act/Bill just for Americans?

You try to tell us we are not allowed to speak out against you. No one tells us here in America what we're allowed to say! You can dislike that all day! Try not to let it keep you awake cuz we ain't changing a f*cking things whether you like it or not.

XXX * XXX

There have been at least 5 "electoral" states lay grounds to sue this election thus far and certain states are starting forensic audits on the election of 2020. When the real votes are counted, and the courts have settled your own stirred up news dust devils. When we're done tabulating the deception and debt there will be a few arrests made. CNN's faces are going to look like you just sucked your own Don Lemon off. You are nothing but a bunch of defectors of America and you are no-longer Americans brethrens. You have no substance or depth, your inkwell is a permanent ink blotter stain that will be judged, annotated, and documented for posterity, and you're going to be on the wrong side of history...

The Honorable President Donald J. Trump is our modern-day martyr-like JFK and MLK. He was chosen by "We The People" who came out in great numbers of 75 to 80 million to elect him while enthusiastic crowds of tens of thousands a day cheered him on. Your disrespectful defiance made us need our President Trump even more, against this Banana Republic! You are the Regulators. You are the Revenuers. You are the Owners, Operators, and Distributors of Equity and all the strings that it pulls!!! You abuse us with our own money! You have no excuse for all the human suffrage. You lack life standers. Americans have had enough of these thieving lunatics with their stiff upper lip, running our government.

This government is in the business of taking! "Legalized Mafia tactics called Regulations!" The government does not make money without our signature on it! The government can not give us anything because the government owns nothing! The government's welfare system is a social chain. You took it from us to put it into these aid program(s). Your's are so rich in privileges, that makes the poor people's problems so annoying. You can't do anything good for us. That we aren't perfectly capable of doing for ourselves! All you do is persecute us, and raise the cost of living. Slobber all over our challengers. Overspend our funds! Bankrupt our country? You are a bad partner that we just don't need!

We are the self-Governed, a Governance of the People, by the People, for the People, and this is the People's Government. You DHgate our strength with fanatic conjecture. You choose to not serve us is a breach of your fiduciary duty. You are not one of us. You do not live in our neighborhoods. You are tributally disconnected facade of survival-ism-linkage. You have an Associate narrative with no relatability to share with the state of mind of the people. In our natural habitat. Everything is broken, and you particularized your pontification, and embellished your ill-qualification. If this partnership is not working. Then it's time to end the long-windedness. You've been here too long and it's past time for you to be gone!!!

America is under an invasion. This has been a planned hostile takeover. They have infiltrated our government as insurrectionists and We The People all feel attacked. Nothing Nasty Nancy, lil' Chucky F*cky, and that piece of Shift aka POS has done turned us against our #1 President. You people are irrational and have rubbed us all wrong. We're like first-time parents that were told he was "illegitimate" when his natural mother and father are standing right here. We say, "Excuse you, Bless your heart dear, we know where our president belongs!!!" Your dysfunction makes us wonder what do you not have held over Trump, that you have to make so much up? But moreover, then that, what do you have on each other and what's really going on?

You drug up a smelly Corpus Delicti "Obama caused to die" in an improper Impeachment with no evidence. You worked in secret and it was all one sided from the Democrat House from the basement of our Capital Building. "It reeked for months," and we paid for you to work on your own made up stories! There is no Habeas Corpus Defense after Obama killed it! Hey dumb a*ses, there was a transcript. Your make believe performance was a stiff on arrival. When our American leader Victoria Nuland chosen "actor and extra" Ukrainian President refused to play your ram through injustice by perjury in your make believe cordium!

You're Exclusionary sh*t could not stand on any grounds of authenticity so that Piece of Shift strung the Impeachment along like a prop. Piece of Shift ad lived and pretended. Your fraudulent statement from a conversation you had not heard. You had no real knowledge of anything you said, as you entered it into the court record. You improvised, dramatized, and performed your gaslighting. Piece of Shift's a drama queen, drag queen, and denial queen and we watched you go off on it, girl. The way your lips pout like a Pekingese schnauzer gnawing on your own ear. You could make a believer out of Congress from nothing but a lie! You've made us all think the Democratic House has been infiltrated by the CIA or Broadway. You may be being slipped a secret second paycheck cuz man, you are working it? It only cost the people 35 million and over 3 months of nothing getting done. What a complete waste of time from congress, for that Cat on a Hot Tin Roof Theater Production from the Democratic House of ill repute Representatives. We The People don't want made-up, make-believe adolescent drama and actors playing Govern-Mental games, and you are out of here!!!

You, Democrats, are communistic dark-rats. The rule of law doesn't mean a damn thing to you. You plotted your scheme, like Pinky and the Brain's diabolically planning to take over the world. The only world we have, and you cannot share?

Trump has snared you in your own rodent trap and beat you at your own High-Tech, Electoral, and Legal Games. Trump has shown you for what you are! You have tarnished our Election Integrity and that's what antiquity will reflect. You need to be Indicted for treason and put away in GITMO just like when you broke the Geneva Convention Treaty and you killed and captured the Jihadi and stripped them naked and tortured the POWs.

These ex-rogue tyrants make their canoodling cost the people billions of dollars. Multiplied by lifetimes of cash extraction experience. You know how to mark it up to the Deficit. That we will all pay for, for decades to come. It's making less and less sense to have you around sucking from our tit you claim is dry, yet you're always fusing for your own udder. You're a Kune Kune piggy with personal advancement problems. Passing out wealth, right here at home, to the rightful heirs doesn't cross your mind. When it comes time for you to spend what is ours you end up with everything. When your way fails why can't we sue you and don't start with the your "diplomatic" bull sh*t when you're a natural-born f*ck-up, and that's what should be on your resume!

You make it to power, you make change your number-one priority. Turnabout is fair game when you spend your whole life gaming the system that you are in charge of. It comes with an endless fountain that flows with the people's cash, that no one will know if just a fraction is missing. You have never met a dollar you didn't like and the more the merrier. When you're the hostess, you always have the mostess. You just send the bill to America to pay.

There is no limit to your generosity and spending outings signed off on by the USA Government. You have no concern about the color of your donor or where your money comes from. When you're filling your treasure chest and Hedge Funds. You'll take your money from anywhere and anyone.

Money gifted to you sure ain't racist. So without over-stating the OBVIOUS, you are just a ruca and your hypocritical promiscuous-ism is really not that confusing. A hoochie mama is a hoochie mama. The only thing left is to negotiate your price.

You're the one who has never known what a day of foraging is. You've never struggled to make it and you have never gone without. You are more than welcome to resend your wealth to level the playing field or you can shut your filthy mouth that you use to berate the people of this earth that you believe can't smite you because you think we are all less than you even if the money coming is from us and it's our "public accounts" that you spend!!!

XXXI *XXXI

In our communities, the cops bash in the door and don't bother knocking. When they leave, they take us with them, "in handcuffs' and they leave our doors hanging off the hinges. Then all the little hood thugs steal our stuff. After we get released with a record that makes it hard to find a job. We slowly slip through the cracks and fall behind...Just another failed statistic on your census.

You flaunt your employment as a public stupe, with a profitable steady salary. It serves you well when you're telling the government ID-ed slaves were to stand in your Human Service Company pauper lines. Where the crime rate is so high, and you are so liberal you would never live here with us.

We would all like to feed you some of your systems-generated waste that's outdated, and you pass out, categorized as govt. subsidy to recipients. We all stood alongside each other as a calico race of distinguished mosaic extremity. In poverty levels of real-life expressionism! That your life will never know. Down here in the inner cities and towns we all live alongside each other regardless of our family DNA or criminal record. We weren't looking all condescending at each other by skin color, sexual orientation, or beliefs. We know that's the govt.'s job to keep track of all of us according to the label you put on us in all your Departments.

Segregation is not in your kids' curriculum or your secured communities. Where your children's food is prepared by a chef and yours are taught inclusiveness. You have cameras and security in your Gated Sector. You have someone to answer your door, and your kids never give out their info. The system can call your attorney before anyone talks to your kids. Divide, prejudge and conquer are only used on the poor.

You're the one that said, "Obama was clean and well-spoken for a black man." Your g-ass called over half of America racist. Your elite a*ses are projecting your own guilt off on us, regular people. You have maid service and a checkered past. You got this sh*t twisted, and you stir the pot. You are pure evil. You and your money are corrupt. We have to say yes-m-master no matter what color we are. If we dispute you, we will get beaten within inches of our lives. It's all part of the mind-subvert from the padrone that keeps us all needy lackeys. We are always out running avalanches, and our lives collapsing in on ourselves, but fighting you is futile. So, we must all be racist if you say we are. SO FALL IN LINE. LEFT-RIGHT, LEFT-RIGHT!

You have the lineage of your heritage with your prodigy pedigrees. You are always telling us about your exceptionalism that comes with high expectations to always come before all of us. You hobnob your highfalutin better way of living in our face to keep us separated by who the supervisors are, and who they delegate over.

You never say anything sensible or constructive that a hat can be hung on. You only come around when you need something, and you have us convinced we need that in our life.

We could get further in a conversation if you didn't call everything "Uuuuuu, what's it called, you know that thing?" Don't you know, everything doesn't have the same name? Ummmmm, you know what I mean? If we were all mind readers, we wouldn't need leaders! You give us all a headache with your feckless in- efficiency, and we'd all get what we wanted, if "poof" like a magician you'd disappear.

You never worry about a thing because the working Americans will regenerate your piggy bank!!! You never stop and ponder where the money comes from. When you withdraw cash from your bank account that's not an expansion to your whole. Emergency Funding is not a wish list, that we all have to buy you everything you want, or else! Years of you wasting and causing debt cannot be used, reconsolidated, and then charged back to us. You cannot extend what you do not have. Throwing good money after bad, to correct the problems means you're not capable of getting an oversight to the variant numbers, of extreme intervals of the fenced concrete jungles, and those displaced people that plague the world.

Your yoga Zen doesn't give you status or increase your assets so it's not a wise investment plan to present to Steve Manutian, who's from Goldman Sachs and would sign anything at an exorbitant increase of the cost. No matter what your price increase does to the 99% majority of the people of the world. You 1%ers won't be put out, you're not going to pay for a thing from your concentrated wealth... But we will and we will have to pay for it no matter what deal you make... HAHAHA, FUCK THE PEOPLE ALL THE WAY TO THE VAULT OF THE ONE-EYED TEMPLE OF MASONRY. THE OLD GREEDY BASTARDS CLUB!!!

That half-empty glass, state of mind you live in, cuz there is only enough for you. And that nice pay increase that you have, that you did not earn with labor. Comes from us paying you to lie to us the only thing you are good at. Erroneously is how you use your words to hide your real intent, despite what the people wanted. Turn around your problem onto your victim is how you play. You are a blame shifter. What you have done, is where your victims lay in restraints for the sh*ty things you thought up. Rules are for little people and you make the rules up as you go along. You contrived these pretentious, fictitious none-newsworthy stories and caused the whole thing to erupt. You embroiled these troubles. The more you defame others, the harder you dig in and hold on you fool, you fool, you fool, how do you live with yourself, and what a wasteful fool you are?

You are void of reality, your depraved pretend life has you so distressed you need a rest. It's hard work keeping up with all your fabricated stories that never really happened. All your loose ends are coming unraveled. You're frazzled, you're losing your razzle-dazzle.

You're always on or off your meds or else you are checking into Betty Ford. Due to your own goat-headedness and obsessive need for more, more, more. You preach down to us, warps our youth. you "Loco Vato." You must have a concussion carrying around that swollen egotistical big ole helium-air-cranium. How do you not just float the f*ck away?

A breakdown to get attention isn't something in an average person's budget. Who's going to pay our bills while we go on vacation on narco-substances drowning Americans by prescription? You can't grasp the simplest of life's concepts. Using one's mind and hands to do good gives internal happiness. So, you can like yourself and who you are. Because when you screw others before they screw you, makes you a big screw fest.

Sine qua non, coup d'état from the crest, prerequisite, planting evidence. The Falus News Station's Family pushes play on what is real. Marqeta gets paid off to never snitch. The silence is so loud it's deafening. Anderson Cooper's holy mother's crucifixion, "of art." and brother's suicide from a 2nd-story. Walls that watch, and ominous paintings eyes that's always on view. You cover up the trap door that leads to your accommodation. A Maze of Catacombs. Stipulated, Summons. Habeas Corpse, Cordon. There's a whole 'nother world to the dark web. Epstein didn't kill himself... Do you hear the whispering voices? Drip, drip, drip goes the little leaks. The punisher creeps. The dark rat runs. The day of the dead, Cibolo Ranch with doors that do not lock, Coto in the middle of nowhere, Advocates of honor killing leave no one to tell no tell. We think you're hiding a lot! Persona non grata. RIP Justice, plagiarism is a totalitarian taskmaster!

We know about Pizza Gates, all your hidden meanings in your symbols, and spirit cooking with Marina Bracavick. You wouldn't have gotten that big leading role at the Big Cinemax if you didn't entertain Weinstein! It's not ok to abuse one's position of power but it's also not ok for me-too-ers to claim to be a victim. When you participated to get what you wanted. It's the oldest profession in the world, and it looks like it paid you well. We get it, GwenJen Dear, you suffer for the arts, but child sacrifice cannot be the golden ticket's going price for the Academy. You would kill for your craft because it happened to you first, is lost on us who care about our kids. Oscar occultation is oculus wide open, and we are seeing 20/20 clear. Your kids have parental restrictions. We see why you people never allow your children to watch television, or have a phone.

The higher you are the harder you fall from importantness. We will hold you individually accountable for everything you thought you got away with. Your gilded cage is about to burn. Ashes to ashes will overtake everyone. Free will is everything and more than you can handle. It puts you in a panic when your control trap gets tested. You are not a people person. It's called acting! You're hallucinating. Your sh*t is all an illusion and you are psilocybin tripping. You repeating yourself does not make it more true. You're heaving and heavy breathing, You're qualmish. You need a straitjacket before you hurt yourself. If you can't get to us. One of your ailments is Trump derangement syndrome. Over your fear of losing your perceived power...

It's time you get your wake-up call! You say we are simpletons when you need us to secure everything that keeps your taarup functioning but in an employment line, you have no real talents to contribute to this world. It takes our elbow grease to keep society functioning like a well-oiled machine.

We wouldn't call you to fix a flat tire or a leaky toilet so please stop telling us how to fix the earth you are not grounded to. You don't know where the water comes from when you turn on the sink or where it drains to when you pull the plug. You think potting soil comes in a bag made by scientists when all it is, is dirt with some dung mixed in. You have hired help, spa days, and you eat where you are served by a maitre-d. You let everyone around you work for you. Stop trying to act your way to your perspective of reality. You are a LARP trying to connect to us. B*tch we ain't homies and we ain't friends so don't cause us to have to protect our hood when we go off on you! You've got no more sense than to go play in the street and you can't figure out why you got run over, ain't even a metaphor dealing with you! IT'S LITERAL!!!

We're climbing out of your Donner Party. Your Cuban soup kitchen. Where shredders, glitchers, hacking B*TCHES, and Swamp Monsters of Smartmatic Domain keep turning the input up and down on the percentile of our pursuit of happiness. We believe our rights are being oppressed and our choices are being made for us in the land of the free. You've taken advantage of us to the point we'll take no more.

We've survived your GENO, GMOs, cloning dolly, test-tube babies, organ transplants, Red Market, Bill Gates profiting with his Family Planning engineering and AIDS for Africans experiment? Who had the USA paying for Mexico's abortions? And was CDC and Gates Foundation Involved? UNFPA sells baby parts! Who knew killing "embryos' is a business! Regeneration Beauty Industry. Now you want to abort full-term babies! WHAT ARE YOU DOING??? Is that human veal? You are diablo baby-eating cannibals! That is so morbide of you, and we don't care what you call it. We're sure our simplicity to your superficial complexity is underwhelming to your expertise and you'll kill all the babies that you want to!!! Rich people call yourselves civilized in your higher pyuria tank? Where we all have to swim to live and you nit-pick us to death.

You scoring and keep track of our CIP, ID, criminal record, medical, blood, credit, taxes, and marriage(s) scares us. With all your consistent proding cause we know we are just a number. We do you no good dead or alive. You look at us like we have an expiration date and it's nearing. We never know who or what's next with you? It will be our surprise.

You are suspected of pirating living donor organs, superbug spreaders, vaccines, and disease manipulation. Why are the "medicines" made with asbestos and petroleum? The new super threat is not even Harp, Jade Helm, or prison camps. You've weaponized our weather and we worry about CERN now. You have shown us your big bridge and tunnel opening in Sweden? Where your goat performed Beastiality, front and center stage with your three-horned gotcho wranglers. Your laborer's death is progress, and progress can not be halted. We are a pedantic workforce for what the elite accomplish.

Hmmm makes us all wonder about Louisiana's levees breaking and flooding out the poor with capsizing tidal waves. We quibble over, whether or not the California wildfires were started by streaks of fireballs falling from the sky? Monsoons, Cloud Seeding, KIM Trails, Sun Flares, pin-point microwave radar, lasers, and superweapons.

Saturn's Hexagon, Cube Belief, and Methane Gas exploration in outer space? UFOs are now UAPs. Declassified files saying we are not alone. You've eng-genetically altered everything we consume with Monsanto, and genetically altered propagation. Vaporized or freeze dried for mass duplication. Agent Orange Dioxin, Over-prescribed Antibiotics, Diazepam, painkillers and Hormones.

You say it's all for overpopulation, and too hard to feed the masses. But we can feed more people on less land than at any other time in history. There's nothing wrong with the old way. No modified and engineered experiments are on your family plate for dinner. But you feed us pink slime burgers and stewed bug soup. Putin doesn't feed his people this crap and they still eat real meat in the Soviet Union! We keep buying your processed products, and you keep pumping them out. We stay in a state of desperate poverty, with poor health. While you are completely out of touch with us.

XXXII * XXXII

Bohemian Grove is a club of apartheid upper-crust privileged M-F*CKERS but you don't really eat people, right? You just drink from the adrenal glands and wear our skin like pelts while you burn baby images, like the Aztec Inca. You May-pole around a eulogy sometimes naked, Nixon said and maybe that's what really made Kissinger mad enough to go after Tricky Dicky with Watergate in the 70's? You say there's nothing wrong with the oligarchy having autonomous meetings. It's harmless fun, and how you bond and make friends. It's so lonely at the top, spending gaggles of other people's money. You think you are the owner and smooth operator of America the Corporation. You dogmatically finagle your authority at the top. You are world leaders who hold high-security clearances to the country you're sworn to under oath and by law. There are Parliamentary, Ethical, and Conductual rules that none of you have followed. You say no one has ever discussed while there elections, Intel, security, laws, land, fractional reserves, and world deals on an international scale, like a One-World Order with one global currency? Weaving spiders need not come here? But no reporters are allowed, and the guest list remains unrevealed to pondering eyes, and "We The People" that put you in office. Seems to us there may be some nefarious underhandedness going on. Maybe some Govt. ACORN, State-Owned Enterprise, Nonprofits, Stalks,CBDC, CDs, IRAs, Trusts. Where one hand doesn't know what the other hand is doing? Call us the slow ones, but isn't it illegal for the wealthiest people in the world and our World Leaders, Financiers, Scientist, Land Barons, Media Moguls, and Diplomats to gather at diabolic gatherings behind closed doors when the public isn't made privy, per se?

How do you work for us when you are a clear sellout!!! You need to be removed from office immediately!!! We thought you weren't supposed to have a faux government that's running the deep state government, that's over the shadow government of the fake government, that's functioning for the government, we thought was the real government that governs over us. And are we paying for all of this?

All of your knowledge, experience, import, export, insider influence, interest earnings, briefings, exchanging this for that, barter, buy, gifting, lifting, diamonds left in your hotel rooms. Your Dubai and Swedish bank accounts seem illegal and swamp-like… At least to the silent majority what you like to call the masses of us commoners! Why can't you do some good with all your eminent domain? We know you will just say we are all too stupid to understand! Well, you sure as hell don't get it and you think you're highly intelligent. Now it is time you spend the rest of your life in Sing, Sing for all your bad faith deals. We'll see how smart you think you are after a few years behind bars?

You all have trusts and estate planning to pay all your bills in-an-inadvertent manner! It's like an agent of the agent from the agency you paid but not "you" directly makes you slick and above the law, you work for. You have this account for that and that accounts for this, makes you look like you aren't involved in anything egregious! "Conflicts of Interest!" Outliers, lie in wait. Embezzling, cheating and stealing you are embedded with the Deep State. No one can question the top of the pyramid that you built. You're scandalous, unscrupulous, and cut from the same cloth... You keep your third eye on Horus- assets. We need not question anything about how our money gets spent. You've already made-up plenty of excuses, to keep us busy and overworked. You keep us frustrated and separated from our own incomes. Jumping through your hoops, according to your standards. Due to your insatiable appetite that can not be satisfied.

You're a wind-up toy that has hit the Great American Wall and it's made you go plum Chinese. The Communistic Democrats are completely corrupt, and you best stand down before you cause a world war. You may find your neck in a nous in a tribunal before the Pristine American Court system brought by the Executor President Donald J. Trump, The United States, and the American people. Our country is our Constitutional Republic, and our Democracy can be applied to you, and this Mutiny of Oompa Loompas.

You're not leader material, no one that's grown wants to follow you!!! Here's a novelty, try getting a f*cking job in the private sector as a kickoff of your future endeavors of saving the earth. At least get off you're a*s and do something, anything, make a difference!!! Any help is better than no help so help someone other than yourself for once!!! Go volunteer just to get some skills!

There is such a thing as too many tattoos, with all that skittle head hair coloring that makes you look like you rode in on Rainbow

Bright's Little Pony, We don't want you up and all personal with our kids and FFS stop parking a junkyard of steel on your face!!! It's hard to take anything about you seriously because grown-ups put their toys away to pay their bills. Good luck making a paycheck because of the signs hung upon oneself? Don't get all pissy when people read it loud and clear. Don't let life pass by like it's in-granny gear. Get up and figure out how to participate and support yourself. Then the government can't tell everyone what to do, but our parents still will, and that's 4-EVER!!! No one will change those Maxum's until we all stop paying taxes!!!

The whole time you're screaming save the children... We are trying to save our children, we are trying to save our children from you!!! We all want to know which one of you lambaste leaders is going to stop molesting, lying, and misleading our children. Who's going to stop the stealing from the next generation? Then come back and report to us how much you care!!! Cause when you speak you are just breathing a lot of hot air.

You have our children doped up on Big Pharma due to a youthful lack of life experience, while they are feeling out one's individual identity. They're not even old enough to legally live on their own and sometimes they need a little reminder.

You exploit their youth by you making your living writing down their names and problems, But you don't help a damn thing! A troubled beginning that may or may not fracture a child's transformation into adulthood needs their parents, parenting not a stranger! Can you get to the root cause of facts, not fantasy! Try working within reality's realm, not your ego's! If you have your knife in the parent's back, you are the problem. Your system suffers from child scapegoat jubilation!!! You are a conflict to our interests. An inept ministry of incumbency.

Your protocol's success depends on our family's defeat!!! Even though you are paid by us!!! You protect our enemy due to your own clash with integratori structure! Your attack on our families is not professional, it's personal!

The CYFD and the DOJ are the number-one family dividers, human traffickers, and drug dealers of the world. We could stop the laboratory narcotic epidemic if we could arrest you!!! Why are the Police and MSM going along with this affray of the elite doping so many people? Aren't you supposed to protect the meekest of us? The Prescriptions that the medical Industry is handed out right and left-right in front of you? Why are you not following up on all the shrinks and Dr's that are legally doping our youth and the elderly? When are you going to figure out where the dope comes from? It may be as close as your own connection!!! These are the issues we elected you to work on, but you haven't gotten anything done. It's the same as it ever was. You are being paid to stop the abuse of power that you are being a participant in. Your system looks like a big circle jerk so don't act like we can't see it!!! We The People have to pay for all this trauma and misery, that is called the govern-MENTAL body that is crazier than all of us. You'll are totally out of touch and heartless

If we could live in peace there would be no victimizing, it's up to us the individual to do what's right on our path no matter where our path leads to. The journey is why we're gifted the vessel. Let's all learn to be kind to one another...And right now it's rudiments to love America, our girl needs us more than ever, and together we will kick these Anti-Freedom, Anti-Liberty, and Anti-American Infiltrators A*S's! Government does not run us! They will stop thinking they are our bosses!!! We will show them we need less Government, not more!!! We need more freedom, more choices, and more voices. Less for you and more for all of us is our new mantra...

XXXIII * XXXIII

THIS DELEGATION'S MOVEMENT IS INDECENT AND UNAMERICAN! We are not ready to pledge to your freak flag just yet, and the way you are acting has made us all want to burn it. Stick that message up your mase and wave it. We do not bow down to your omnishambles unit! You are unfurling your discordancy off on us. Your plight has no moral boundaries and is unconscionable. Your snobbery with your better than thou contention is in opposition to our demonstrative brave girl! "Old Glory!" You better know her name stands for triumph over tyranny! You better know her story of sacrifice and gain. Her stars and stripes represent her mercy and grace. When we stand and pledge allegiance to her in the sanctity of protections by her shield of armor. She is an honored emblem to the world that is a symbol of the American people's independence. We are created with endowed aspirations by solvent human beans! Who has sovereignty over rulers' doctoring. An endearing ember that's warm and burns in the heart of the whole world for freedom, faith, and family. That gives rein over your monarchy fraudsters. Unshackled restraints make our girl great like our Statue of Liberty. Don't you dare tell us that we are to take down our country's banner that rings with equity, equality,and liberty for all! We, us, our's are her people who are willing to kill and die for her and what she stands for. Our divine rights are fragile and precious when they are like no others! Our innate spirits are specific to raising hell and charter. Our distinctive benefaction needs nurtured for prosperity. We spend our lives protecting her generation after generation to give the gift of self-ownership to our children. America's Old Glory is a love story that's going to give what's asked of her.

Righteous Indignation and unruliness is not our style. Once you have been exposed to truth and experienced America's Republic you will long for her shores forevermore. No one will turn out that passionate love lights whose toll is carried on by those who dare to follow in the Dawning of a Free Nation and all her Grandeur.

Anyone that crosses our girl, her working-class people, and her arm- bearing militias, will meet our fury, wrath, and the resurrection of 1776. We The People of America will rise to do it again!!! Don't make us have to go Alex Jones on you. We have the numbers that can conquer the 1% to topple your dictatorship when we are 99% strong in unified solidarity. We The People of America are her Regime. By our Bill of Rights it's time you hear our roar! We will be loud, and we will be proud because that is the American way. We will spell it out to you, FORTY-FIVE WILL NOT CONCEDE!!!

Those that are on your side are equal in corruption regardless of political affiliation! You have never fooled us. You silenced us like communistic China! We have known all along our government is corrupt and this is not new news to us so stop with the deception and barrenness. You have lost your benevolence. You are disingenuous and you are not engaged with us. You can't see what's right in front of your face. To quote the words of the famous Cat Williams, "N****, we're sitting right here!"

Once we find out where your loyalty lies and your profits come from. A lot of you will need to vacate your political seat and your political career. You will be sitting on your kidney and prostate, making license plates if we have our way. You have run our earnings down to minus zero by the time we're done paying you each week. We have to show you where our pennies go. Now we would like to Militarily audit all your finances. Where's your commerce attached to, and where does that rabbit hole go? Was it personal or corporate? When you own the government, those lines are so vague! Hillary said in 2015, "If Trump wins, all of you will hang." Knowing what we know in 2021 we're sure that's over half of you. It's time to clean OUR HOUSE and get rid of the entangled old spiderwebs! You are the same old politicians every election that has already run our country into the debt we're in! Your prudence has not whitewashed a thing and it's time you leave whether you like it or not!!!

If you have to suck your Jell-O through a straw, you are probably too old to legislate. We The People must stop putting up with stale snacks, missed naps, and aggravated seniors in our government employment. This may be elder abuse? With all your cognati decline you shouldn't be making choices that the rest of us have to live with. So put a feed bag on you and put you out to pasture like senile Depends-wearing Maxine and Nadler.

You're clunkers with no clutch, and stuck in acclimation to an agenda. The more things change the more things stay the same, as you sell us out again, and again. A cult of high finance. You want everyone to worship you. Acquisition by force. You have the final say over us. You want our Independence taken away. We have no say about the choices you make for us. We have come last, with you behind the wheel. You drove the people into poverty like you think you are JP Morgan. You're a sad leader of contention in your nocentism and non-advancement, sealed with your official letter head on it, as you diddle with diplomacy. No one is impressed by you or your caucus. Why do we put up with these old grieves? You showing out, is your engine stalling. Your slipped tranny is a hoopty that only runs backwards. You have a piston stuck up your a*s's from festering so much internally. You are a library of traitor Joe secrets. It's time you release it and just let it go. No one should have to work for over 65 years straight, screwing over We The People. All the way up and into your early 80's and 90's. You have never had any other career. Congress needs an age cap, not a nightcap, where you sleep it off in your Government Office. Anyone that has to serve a life sentence to Moloch the long in the tooth Owl God has been a pundit way too long.

Your Higher Power is blasphemous. You are brackish and distasteful. Did you forget we pay you with your Dr. Phordian Psychopathy, Ph.D.'s. Masters of temperature Degrees who are always cool cucumbers in control. You are a Northern blown snow Globe and Ice Fairy is your name. You judge us while your urban fortresses are deep underground shadow states for the untouchables. We say we want change, so you rearrange the same old plays. What a game this is to you! Different day, same old bull sh*t, one election right after the other!

XXXIV * XXXIV

Trump has never been an Attorney General, District Attorney, Legislature, Judge, or Lawmaker. Trump never has written the public laws that take our babies, sons, and daughters away or dispose of our brothers, husbands, and fathers! Shackles, chains, and handcuffs. Cold prisons with one blanket. Cement floors and the lights left on all night. We got no money to put on our books for commerce. Poor families that don't have a car to travel to see their loved ones on visitors' day. Who's supposed to know their parents when you locked them away?

Trump has never separated any American families and Trump didn't start any new wars. We The People have no personal beef with him. We all want to rally with him, and the more you lie about him just shows us what imposters you are! We can see who works for us. If you need to know why we like Trump, it's because you repulse us so much. President Trump brought his own security to the White House so he wouldn't be assassinated by our own rogue CIA that couldn't protect the Twin Towers or John Kennedy Sr. We wouldn't want another FBI hitman to get promoted to vice and presidential statues, receive 72 virgins in heaven for murdering here on earth or to be tragically Oswalded.

President Trump has done in one term what you could not do in decades. He donates his salary to charity, and he paid his own way through his campaign. He severed his profits and authority to his own businesses. He did not capitalize on his power, with insider trading and he did not gain at our loss. His children are not on meth, and they have careers and go to work every day. They do not need to make their money in nymphomaniac ways like you sluts that sell out your own country!!! The Democrats are killing Democracy!!!

Trump made the EPA clean our drinking water that Bush and Obama was caught funneling out of the DOD trust funds. Trump brought our jobs back from across the seas that you said were never going to return and he did it without a magic wand, "Barakamon." President Trump gave to the Black Colleges, increased the Blacks' sectors Employment and exemplified the Black Ministers, Preachers, and Teachers, and encompassed the black family. Trump knows the worth of the mothers and fathers that bring up the babies and raise the children that grow up to marry our sons and our daughters to start a family of our own.

President Trump cut the regulations stagnating our industries. Steel, oil, mining, and logging are back in business again which makes American completely Independent and Dependent on no other country. Why does China own Tik Tok that takes personal identities, iCloud that stores our info, computers, printers, intel, spyrear, 3rd party voting machines, solar panels, batters, and everything else in manufacturing? Why does China make our medicines? Do they hold title and ownership to our shipping dockyards in Long Beach? What happened to the pride of the USA label on it? Which one of you thought selling out America was a good idea? You're fired!

He seeded a friendship with rocket man, and you never would have done that. He brought the Israel capital to Jerusalem. He made peace in the Middle East and that no man has ever done since the written word. The treaty between Israel and Palestine has welcomed Iran with an olive branch to try to achieve world peace. Why wouldn't you want that?

President Trump's negotiations brought the prices of the medicines down so old people don't have to choose between food or their prescriptions. He took on Big Pharma who could not be sued over their flu shots since Reagan was in office. He's opened the White House up to the regular people and brought corporate heads in to stimulate our supply and demand, which is basic civics and economics. The only reason you would stagnate our supply chain is if you want to drive up the prices! He stared down the static from the nonsense, non-news reporters every day. MSM could not break The Donald.

President Trump strengthened our depleted military, hoping to never use it. He wants to bring our troops home, but you all would have none of it. He got us out of the UN Delegation that stopped us from being the world's police and welfare system. Maybe we could see some of our own money put back into our economy, infrastructure, and America's people. He stopped the trade embargoes and put tariffs on incoming goods and taxed leaving industries. Trump made us, American Strong and tight as a drum-like Harley Davison "Made In America."

45 has the most beautiful wife, Melania. The magazines and fashion world lost their minds and snubbed her! Whores judged her modeling history. You refused to show off our First Lady of Honor. You would not dress her or put her on printed covers. Your prejudiced choices against our American Contessa have shamed your own sham of the textile industry. Maybe men that want women to look like unhealthy young boys shouldn't tell women what looks good?!? Your toxic cancerous vanity has no redeeming qualities, and youth or beauty aint safe around you! Now you think we want to look at the toads from the Bud beer commercials as centerfolds!

We don't have a king and queen born to a monarchy that we have to support for doing nothing but hailing with a stolen scepter. We Have an Honorable First Lady and a President with Authority as the Highest General of the Regiment. We like and elect him by the people that legally live here. We The People back him and our Great Country Over you, feeble-minded dictators that are snakes and rats. We are all tired of being cheated by you! For the first time in decades, we love our President and respect his Politics. You'd be wise to not come to stabour FLOTUS and POTUS in the back and they best stay safe, or you are going to pay the price prescribed by law. President Trump will carry out the removal of ex delicto swamp gadders of both parties. Trump's going to drain the swamp and resistance is feudal.

He is our favorite President, Muy Bueno Senior. He has had the atonement to be a leader we can look up to. He should have won three Nobel Peace prizes but your financial influence amongst the affluence has such a great reach when you donate to the coffers you can even distort distinguished Academia.

You can't stop the swearing-in of an Honorable SCOTUS to the Supreme Bench of the law of our land. The courts belong to all of us and you're going to need SCOTUS when we're done spanking you. Then you will need a little time out, on Rikers Island. President Trump has been the president you wish you could have been. We are a land of Honor with the Distinction of Freedom. We are proud people with natural progression and setbacks. These things are what bind us all together regardless of ethnicity, education, or philosophy. We don't live where one side takes all nor does one person have all the control and power. We have common-sense rules and written trespass restraints that apply to all. We have protocol and procedure. We weigh both opposing opinions by law, law, law, keeps the peace, and makes us all equal.

We can petition our government. We have equal access to the law, the right to redress any grievance, freedom to petition in court or by peaceful protest, and the right to be secure in our person and property. We have rights to own and open carry. The Second Amendment "SHALL" not be altered. It's our first defense against a tyrannical government and we are like no other country for it. Now you know why everyone wants to live here! And David Chappelle said the Second Amendment is in case the first one doesn't work out…

XXXV * XXXV

We've elected minorities to every Department, Agency, and Office. If you can't see that, then you aren't looking hard enough. You see what you want to see in your prism. We aren't going to ride that dead horse ever again. It's mental and non-systemic. If you are but 11% of a whole, giving you half would not be fair to anyone else and you damn sure aren't getting a 100%. Everything in life is not served up to you on a silver platter, just because you ordered it. No one is your servant. It's time you start giving back is the lesson you best learn because none of us owe you a damn thing!

The insults that you sling about our alignment with Trump show how incomplete and empty that you are. You're just a shell of a person hiding behind your heisted power through your threaded bloodline, fraternity letter, or computer screen. You act like you're better than us. You get your strength from being cruel and having too much has gone to your head. You walk across the little guy to get to where you are going but toe to toe with any man or woman, you're a mouse of a human bean.

We are a multi-creed nation of every genealogy range of Homo sapien, and then some. How much more diverse could we be? In every war we've ever fought we stood alongside each other regardless of colors. We had each other's back no matter who our ma and pa were. Color did not stop us from being each other's brothers and sisters on the battlefield and color does not stop us from being each other's brothers and sisters in peacetime. Arm and arm we stand together in antipathy and resistance to our common enemy. We are our brothers' and sisters' keepers. We are red, white, and blue patriot- loving, firearm toting, militia-fighting warriors, and America and her colors do not run. How do you like Frances Scoot Key's, Star- Spangled Banner, now! We are only as free as our neighbors so no matter who our neighbors are, just know we got our 6. We are about to rumble, and you best go get you an OJ's dream team cause you ain't going to buy your way out of this. You have done gone off and pissed us all off and we may liberate a country or two before we're done with you cause everyone wants what we got, and we aren't willing to give what is ours up to you.

Freedom is not free, a Republic does not come without a vigil, and bondage has never been broken without taking a stand. Our country's father George Washinton who crossed the Delaware December 25, 1776 to start a fire in the belly of the world that had never been seen before or sense. That freedom jewel is a voice born inherently inside of every person on this globe and our freedom is what makes America's value shine out to the world. We've all been endowed with the rights of blue blood nobility just by living here in this great land. No one in America wants to hold us back from being all we can be.

We can challenge the law and even change the law. We have the right to our choice in counsel, Freedom of Speech, Bear Arms, Stand

Our Ground. We speak our minds, and we're grown so we can let you have a voice too. We have the right to protect our familia and property. We don't have to take any sh*t from no one! We have the right to choose our faith and religion, make up our own if we so choose. You can be Spiritual, or an atheist. You can be secular or reject all of it. Try that in another country and we would never see you again.

You can live here and be an entitled antagonist and tread on the backside of our belief even though we are the most versatile country of them all. We've fought for your right to disrespect our flag that our ancestors died for. Our girl "Old Glory" has been resilient in strength, forgiveness, and she's a World Class Beauty. That everyone aspires to "she's adorable," and she makes us all proud to live here when she flies in honor of our patriotism.

We welcome constructive discourse as long as you are on point, proper, and don't cause violence. We have everything that a person could want, and we don't want to live anywhere, but where we are. We are rabble-rousers, where we have already severed ties from tyranny to taxing, to form our own "Free Nation. " Tea Party Holdouts." This is our land, our home where our flag stands for who we are, and you got no respect, you best get to moving along while you can!

We have human rights, workers' rights, and equal protection, equal access to our law, is extended to every person legally in her jurisdiction, "including our President." You can't understand that you may be the stupid one. You call us ignorant because we want our inheritance and our rights that are endowed to us by our maker and Constitutionally scribed by James Matison to the grantee by the grantor, our conquering forefathers. Thomas Jefferson forged our Declaration of Independence. We have everything we need deeded and documented as well as our brazing fortitude being born inside of us instinctively. The pineal fingerprint of life, liberty and freedom cannot be stolen, broken or killed. So, if you keep writing repetitive laws for laws we already have, we will have to believe you can't find the first ones. You have no business writing law at all?

You're in contrast with nature and our rights. Now clean up and out this Regulatory mess! We need less of you minding our business, not more, and if you fear us, GOOD!

XXXVI * XXXVI

We have checks and boundaries for you legal Officials. Attorney General, Inspector General, Dept. of Justice, Secretary of State(s), Foreign Affairs, Intelligence, Homeland Security, DOJ, HHS, and all Cabinet members. With the National Guard, Army, Navy, Marines, Air Force. Police, State Police, Sheriff's Dept., Marshalls, Texas Rangers, Governors, and Mayors. You better step up to the line that's being drawn before all of you. You better wake up out of the coma you've been walking around in no matter how woke you think you are because this is bigger than just this Nation.

We are starting to believe you are one of them or you have been sleeping on the job! While you was looking out for your own job security you let the thieves come in and they are holding America's democracy hostage. Where's the intelligence on these F*ING TRAITORS!!! The DOJ, CIA, and FBI are total tool Departments. Alphabet Cereal-Killers in Federal Offices that Duc Decoma subpoenas can't get your files and records released or they will all be redacted. The military may need to be dropped in to take them! Where is the Durham Report and has, he gone F*cking AWOL? Safe Harbor Day deadline is but a rule, constitutionally superseded and arbitrary. The GOP did not inaugurate Biden on Dec. 08, 2020, giving us all hope that the McConnell's RINO's might do what's right for your country and fight for us. But "Professionals" don't go against your own, and you all have your own skeletons so there's no one to stop The Great American 2020 Election Steal by these Anti- American Malo Amino Malicious Tortfeasors?

Congress, Supreme Court, State District Court, Administrative Electoral, Assessors Offices, why are you so quiet? Do you only care about your own rubles? Do you have no scruples? ARE YOU NOT

HUMAN? What happened to the golden rule that you are "Legally Required" to not stand by and watch crimes being committed? Your failure to act is a failure to the people of America. You are obligated by law so don't tell us the court, can't see it. If you refuse to investigate a crime, obviously you can't see it! Obstruction of Justice, Abuse of Power, Malicious Abuse of Prosecution, Election Fraud, on and on and on! "The court can only see the law" Then take your blinders off and get your job done!

These are your peers and bigger than overseeing the civilian people!!! This is High Treason and a Terroristic attack on our country! This is your job title's duty to protect and serve! Authenticity is your Ethical Oath, not cover-ups and blocking the wishes of the people! A cheater is not a winner, nor a leader. Real Americans are asking, who's going to prison? You are the arbiter of law and the enforcement, Maria Carta, you serve the people, not these criminal organizations and these bosses of the United Corporation of America!

Mayor Rudy Giuliani, Judicial Watch, One American News, and Epoch has been on this ongoing plight to right the rights of our girl. Her furry and the Kraken have been released by Sidney Powell Esq. and Mike Lindell, My Pillow Guy is ready to Ombudsman the world, America is not your personal money printing machine, and you need to start paying for these damages you have caused. We'll see you down here in purgatory with us, in the lower income tax bracket. America will correct your lawlessness, injustice, and indemnification is the relief Americans seek from you well to do winches.

Vice. Prez. Elect, and illegitimate Prez. Bidens whose victory margin is fraudulent. You will not be offered fortitude for what you have stolen. Deceivers will not win and a champion you will never be. Fair is fair and what's good for us is good for you. JUSTICE IS NOT TWO-TIERED!!! The world can see you and we will show the world that no one is above the law when we imprison you as you have imprisoned us. You will be made an example of why not to mess with America!

If there is a breach in command and any RINO, GOP in Congress may be compromised like McConnell, McCarthy, Graham, Romney, and Chaney. You fist bump in an unwritten treaty across the bow of saboteurs. Your Orwellian fear-mongering is not our ideal of assembly of order. You declare war on America and her people, we'll Indemnify the Bataille of you and yours, regardless of your rank or affiliation.

You try putting your plant in our highest executive office, you come to try to take our county or our Presidential seat. "We the People," in vast swells of numbers too considerable to count, will resurrect the Great American Valeant Spirit in her "mutts." WWG1WGA...

We shall Reconsolidate our American Union. We The People will stand with each other and hold the line against you traitors. We The People elected President Trump on Nov. 3, 2020. We will not stand down to you. We will not be silenced by you. We will not forget. We will not forgive. We will be defiant, and we will dishonor these intruders to our Land and Home.

We will fight your tyranny as our forefathers have taught us. The United State of America's Constitution Reign Supreme, here in the land of the free. Where dictators crumble, and We The People rule the rulers, and our elections are handled democratically. Wealthy nobility does not have righteous indemnity. You best Barr-down and resign if you know what's good for you. We will match your shield of armory against the might of our heart.

If you come and try to take what was born inside all of us and nurtured by our Republic domicile of individual rights.... We The People will victoriously restore our girl's honor, and liberty crown. One Nation, Indivisible. Where our red, white, and blue waves! The home of the brave. We know our girl's worth, and you will know when we are done with you, that all the wealth of the world will buy you nothing round here! America, her nonconformist, and freedom loving people are not for sale! She belongs to our children, and our children's children Lock, Stock, and Barrel!!!

TEXAS
FOR TRUMP

www.ingramcontent.com/pod-product-compliance
Lightning Source LLC
Chambersburg PA
CBHW070125260726
48658CB00001B/265